DEDICATION

To my wife Angela for her unfailing support and encouragement.

Driven to Downing Street

PETER SMITHSON BEM

Copyright © 2014 Peter Smithson

All rights reserved.

ISBN: 1499599676
ISBN-13 : 978-1499599671

CONTENTS

	Acknowledgments	i
1	My Early Years	1
2	Growing Up in London	8
3	My Service in the RAF	14
4	Life after the RAF	32
5	Early Years in the GCS 'Pool'	38
6	Gaining Experience	46
7	Allocated Driver to John Hare (Minister of Labour)	62
8	Driving Lord Drumalbyn (Minister of Pensions) and First Introduction to Margaret Thatcher	67
9	Life in the Fast Lane. Richard Crossman (Secretary of State for Health)	77
10	Highs and Lows with Richard Wood (Minister for Overseas Development)	90
11	Troubled Times with Reg Prentice (Minister of Education)	99
12	Living the High Life. Lord Gromwy Roberts (Minister of State at the Foreign Office)	102

13	Allocated to Sir Geoffrey Howe (Chancellor of the Exchequer)	113
14	Trials and Tribulations in Miami	124
15	Ambition Achieved – Driving Sir Geoffrey Howe (Foreign Secretary)	126
16	The Brighton Bomb	137
17	Living with the I.R.A. Threat	142
18	Sir Geoffrey Howe's Dismissal from the Foreign Office	156
19	House of Lords	161
20	Retirement	170

ACKNOWLEDGEMENTS

I would like to thank Lord and Lady Howe and their family for many kindnesses since I have met them and for their encouragement and help with this book.

I would also like to thank Lady Holderness, who first encouraged me to write my autobiography and gave me guidance along the way.

Finally, without my wife Angela's contribution in editing and typing the manuscript and her constant encouragement and support, this book would not have been possible.

1 MY EARLY YEARS

The crowds cheered as we stepped outside No. 11 Downing Street. I blinked as a mass of cameras flashed when the Chancellor, Sir Geoffrey Howe, held up the battered red despatch box, which had been used to hold the Budget speech since Gladstone's time. It was the big day. The Chancellor was all set to present his first Budget to the House of Commons.

There was always a set routine. After I had parked the official car in its allotted space outside No.11, the door would open to let me in. Gathered in the front hall was the Chancellor, Lady Howe and some of his staff. Placed in one corner was a television set, which we watched intently until the image of the door of No.11 flashed up on the screen. Immediately, Dennis Davey, Sir Geoffrey's messenger and Doorman, opened the door and Sir Geoffrey and Lady Howe stepped outside, followed by his staff and stood on the doorstep. Sir Geoffrey held up his traditional red box to the crowds and cameramen.

At that time, the public were allowed into Downing Street, although the top 25 yards were reserved for the press and TV cameras. As I stood there for a moment, my mind went back to my childhood, living with my grandparents in that little mining village in Durham, and I marvelled at how I'd come such a long way since then.

As Sir Geoffrey lowered the box, I had to walk around the car to the driver's side, and open the rear door for Lady Howe. Meanwhile, Dennis was opening the door on the other side for Sir Geoffrey and his secretary to get into the car. We drove slowly down a packed Downing Street full of cheering crowds into Whitehall and onto the House of Commons. Things had certainly changed around Downing Street in the many years I had been in the Government Car Service since I started in 1956, when the Chancellor would simply walk from No. 11 to the House of Commons, carrying his red box. But then of course, so much had changed.

My mother and father (who I called Mam and Dad) had both moved down from the north of England during the Depression in 1929 looking for work. Dad had come down from Newcastle upon Tyne, with a brother called Edward. After a while they both got jobs with Croydon Council as dustmen but managed to train in their spare time to become bricklayers.

My mother was a nurse when she met my father at a dance hall in Croydon, Surrey, in 1929 and they eventually got married in 1931 and I was born in 1933 in Caterham, Surrey. At that time Mam and Dad had been living in a very small ground floor flat in a house in Purley but Dad managed to get us into a house that had just been built close by. Many years later Dad told me that when we moved into this new house, the builder had offered to sell him the house for £250 or £25 deposit and the rest paid weekly. Dad told the builder he didn't have £25 and the builder then said, "Okay, I'll give you the deposit." But Dad still turned him down!

We were living in Purley but my father could see that it looked as though there was going to be a war with Germany. So when the Second World War started in 1939 and we were living close to three RAF airfields; Croydon, Kenley and Biggin Hill, my parents decided to send me to live with the grandparents on my mother's side at a small village called Etherly Dean, near Bishop Auckland, County Durham. They lived in a miner's cottage, with no gas and only an outside tap and outside toilet. My grandfather was an ex-miner who suffered with silicosis and I remember clearly that he was always out of breath.

At that time I always seemed to be suffering with a very sore throat. The local doctor advised that I should have my tonsils removed but my father would not agree to this. Three doors down from my grandmother's house lived a lady called Mrs Eisen, who was a spiritualist and if anyone died she would lay them out ready for burial. Her husband, who was a local miner, told us that she was always talking to the dead. One day he said, "I didn't get much sleep last night. She was chatting to the spirits in the bedroom half the night!"

She was always dropping in to see my grandparents and on one occasion when she visited, I was in bed with a very sore throat. She had a look at me and said, "I can fix that!" Looking at my grandmother she continued, "Tonight I want you to give him a scarf, which he has to put around his neck himself. Nobody must help him. In the morning he must take it off and put it into the brown paper bag that I'm going to give you." This I did, exactly as she wanted.

The next day she picked up the paper bag with the scarf inside and took it to a lady in the next village who was known as a healer. We were told later that she took the scarf out of the bag and held it for a few minutes before making up a concoction which she poured into a small bottle. Two days later, Mrs Eisen arrived back at my grandparents' house, where I was still suffering with my very sore throat. She handed me the tiny bottle and said I must take out the stopper and drink the whole contents in one go. This I did but how I managed it I do not know as it was unbelievably bitter. Fortunately I managed to keep it down. The next day my sore throat had gone and to this day, I have never suffered with a sore throat again! Some years later when I was about to leave the village, I went to see Mrs Eisen and she took off a pair of brass candlesticks from her mantelpiece and said, "Keep these polished and I will always be there to look after you." I still have them to this day!

Grandad was a bookie's agent, or 'runner' and I would sometimes accompany him to the local pub and sit outside. If the police drove by and pulled up, he would pass the betting slips to me and I would run out of the backdoor and make my way home. In those days betting was illegal but you were safe as long as you were not caught with the betting slips on you.

I went to my first school at Everley, which was over a mile away over the fields. I used to go on my own, which was a bit scary for a young boy of five or six years old, as a lot of the fields had cows in them. Unfortunately, due to the war my education was very much interrupted and it was my wonderful grandparents who taught me to read and do basic number work.

Where we lived, there were only fourteen houses, and no children of my age to play with, so I persuaded my grandfather to let me have a dog. When we bought him, he was only a few weeks old and I called him Rex. He was a little terrier, a bit like a Jack Russell and he became my life and went everywhere with me. When I used to come back from school he would be waiting for me at the end of the lane as I walked home. If I decided to walk down to the river and have a paddle, he would follow me in. He even slept with me at the bottom of my bed. Then one day, I suffered one of the worst experiences of my life as a result of two of my cousins coming to live with us.

My grandparents' eldest son was in the Army and serving in the Middle East. He wrote to my grandmother to say that he had not heard from his wife, who lived in Croydon, South London, for some time. As they had two children, the eldest boy John, five years old, and his sister Wendy, about three years old, he wanted to know if they were alright. My father was asked to go to their address and to find out what was happening. When my father arrived at the house and was knocking on the door a neighbour approached him and said, "She's not in there, but they are" and then pointed to an upstairs window. As there were no curtains, he could see plainly two faces looking down at him. Their hair was matted and down over their shoulders to their waist. My father immediately called the police who broke into the house and found them in a terrible state. However, they looked much better once they were cleaned up, but neither could talk nor understand what was said to them. Their mother appeared to have had a complete mental breakdown and had locked them in an upstairs bedroom, where they had had no contact with anybody nor seen any animal. They couldn't even speak. Subsequently, the authorities put the mother into a hospital.

My grandparents agreed to take the two children in to live with us. I remember that it was a Saturday when they arrived. The whole family were waiting to greet them as they walked into the room. The boy, John, spotted my dog which was sitting next to me and started screaming. No matter how we tried, we could not calm him down and I was told to take Rex outside. About an hour later, I tried to go back into the house, but once again John started screaming. So I was told to stay the night with my dog at a neighbour's house. The next morning, my grandparents told me that they had made the decision to give Rex away. I begged them not to, but a few days later a man arrived with a horse and cart and my little friend was put onto it and tied to a rail. That was the last I saw of my little dog. To this day, I can still remember the look in Rex's eyes as he disappeared up the lane with the rag and bone man. I can't explain how I felt when he was put into the cart and taken away. Suffice to say I was heartbroken and to this day I still think fondly about my little friend.

In 1943, I went to live in Newcastle on Tyne, as Dad had found work at Vickers Armstrong making guns and Mam went to work in a munitions factory. I started at the first of three schools I would attend as I was obliged to keep changing school, because people who had been bombed out of their homes had to be housed in them instead. During this time, I persuaded my father to take in a stray dog, which was very good-natured. But unfortunately, one evening, we all went to the cinema, leaving the dog at home. On our return, when we went into the sitting room, we discovered that the dog had completely destroyed our feather settee. All that was left was a wooden frame. My father got rid of the dog the next day and it took a few more days to get all the feathers cleared up!

I have always been very fond of animals and was to have several more dogs over the years. But at this time, I adopted a rather unusual pet, a one week old chick, which I had bought at the market. The house we lived in only had a backyard, so I made a kind of hutch with a wire cage to keep my chick in. The problem was that he became bigger and more aggressive, as he was obviously a cockerel. However I used to play with him every day and he would let me pick him up and come and eat out of my hand and sit on my knee, but he would attack anyone else that came into our backyard. He became so aggressive that my father sold him to a neighbour who, I believe, had him for dinner. Later, when I returned to London, where we had a small back garden once again, I made a run and bought a little chick, but this time got a hen, who I called Gracie. When she became fully grown, I would go up to the hen house every morning and she would have laid an egg for my breakfast.

It was at about this time that my young five-year-old sister Doreen contracted diphtheria. The authorities came round and put a big yellow cross on the door and windows of our house to let people know to keep away as it was very contagious. There were so many cases that you weren't able to ring the hospital, and so Mam would have to get the newspaper and look for Doreen's number to see if she was on the 'dead', 'serious' or 'getting better' list. Luckily, Doreen recovered.

The road we lived in was very steep and went down towards the river Tyne. I remember one day standing on the steps outside our house watching the German Luftwaffe bombing the ships and the Vickers Armstrong factory on the river Tyne. Once the Germans had dropped their bombs, they had to turn very sharply, which meant that they passed very low over our house. In fact, when they passed over us they were so low we could see the crew clearly, looking at us as they passed over. No sooner had they gone than we saw a British fighter, I think it was a Spitfire, following it. We heard machine-gun fire and then a very loud bang. We got to the crash site as quickly as we could, but the Home Guard were already there and we weren't able to get our souvenirs that time.

Life was pretty tough going in Newcastle. You would be lucky to get through the week without getting into a fight, usually over next to nothing. I remember the first fight I had was with the school bully. I was playing football with a group of boys from our class when this lad, who was much bigger and taller than anyone in the school, grabbed the football and defied anyone to take it back. As it was in fact my football, which I had been given for my birthday and was very hard to obtain as there was a war on, I demanded it back. Soon all the boys standing around started chanting, "Fight, fight", as lads do. He walked over to me and started pushing me around and then punched me very hard in the chest and said that the ball now belonged to him. I was very angry and punched him full on his nose. He went down and was bleeding quite badly as we both rolled around on the ground. He kept shouting, "I'm going to kill you". I was amazed that most of the boys were shouting in his favour. Things were getting a bit out of hand when a teacher grabbed him and took him away. I picked up my football and went back to my classroom. Next day I went to school expecting the worst with the bully waiting for me. However, when I saw him, he just looked away and never bothered me again.

2 GROWING UP IN LONDON

In late 1944, we moved back to London, Kennington where we had a basement flat, which consisted of two rooms, a kitchen and an outside WC. As my father was a bricklayer, he was given the job to repair bombed houses for the many homeless people. Once more, I started a new school, again a pretty tough place. We had two or three teachers who were very good, but there were also a couple of teachers who I would call sadists as they would cane you for next to no reason. I was once caned simply for coughing and was given two strokes of the cane on each hand so hard that both hands bled, and I still have the scars today. But the worst teacher was the Deputy Head. He was a small, fat man called Schmidt, who seemed to get great pleasure from using the cane.

One day, our school team had been playing football in Kennington Park and by the time we returned to school it was just before afternoon playtime. Mr Schmidt had made a new rule that no boys were allowed in school during the morning or afternoon playtime. So when we got back to school, we all rushed into our classrooms to change out of our wet football kit. A young lad called Charlie Onn, who was half Chinese, and myself were stopped by the PT teacher and told we must first clean the boots and do the dubbing of the football. We did this as quickly as possible, but by the time we went back into our class the bell had rung for playtime. Charlie and I were trying to get out of our wet kit and get dressed, when the classroom door flew open, and there stood Mr. Schmidt. He started ranting and shouting at us and would not listen as we tried to explain why we were there.

I then noticed that he had his beloved cane in his hand as he said that the punishment for this misdemeanour would be six strokes each on the backside. He called Charlie over to him and made him bend over a desk. Unfortunately, Charlie had been a bit slow getting changed and still had his wet shorts on. Schmidt started caning and was really laying it on. After the second stroke I saw blood running down Charlie's leg. As I was now wearing my underpants and trousers, I quickly put a couple of exercise books down my pants. When he finished with Charlie, he called me over for my turn. I tried once more to explain why we had been there, but he wasn't interested and kept swishing the cane. He put me over the desk, and I felt the sting as the cane came down. Luckily, the first four strokes were high, but the next two were low and hit the tops of my legs. The pain was unbelievable and I knew that I, too, was bleeding. After the last stroke, Schmidt just turned and walked out of the classroom.

That afternoon I went home and sat at the table, whilst my mother served the meal. She noticed that I was not sitting still for very long and asked what was wrong with me. I reluctantly told her that I had been caned on the backside. She then insisted that I showed her where I had been caned. As I was showing her, my father came in from work. When he saw the state of the tops of my legs he just 'flipped'. I have never seen him so angry. "Right", he said, "I'll take you to school tomorrow. You just point out Schmidt to me." So the next day he accompanied me to school and as we went into the main hall, Schmidt was standing by the swing doors. As soon as he saw my father he knew he was in trouble, but my father was on to him before he could run. He grabbed the teacher by the neck and hit him very hard. Schmidt went through the swing doors, slid along the floor and then lay very still. My father walked over to him and said, "If you cane my son again. I will be back and finish you off." Dad turned to me and said, "I'm off to work now," and left the school. I thought to myself, "I'm really in for it now," but nothing more was ever said.

I was always keen to learn at school, although our class teacher seemed more interested in football. However, during the years I was at school, I often came top of the class. This wasn't because I was brilliant, but simply that the other boys weren't particularly interested in learning. My best subjects were science, metalwork and woodwork, which served me well in later life.

At that time we were living in a basement flat in No.66, Richbourne Terrace and times were very tough and my family had little money. My father and his brother tried to start their own business doing building repairs and decorating. However, as you had to get a permit for any work over £10, they soon went out of business. Nevertheless, my father eventually found a job on the railways as a loader at Nine Elms Goods Yard.

It was at about this time that I managed to get hold of an old pram, which I had found dumped on a bomb site. I wanted to help my family in some way, so I made it into a trolley that I used to take to the Gas Works at Nine Elms on the corner of Vauxhall Bridge. Once a week at 6.30, I would queue up to get a 6 penny bag of coke. Together with the wood I found on the bomb sites, it helped to keep us warm in the winter time.

In particular, I remember clearly Christmas Eve 1947. It was a very cold morning, Mam and Dad had no money to put in the gas meter and the food cupboard was bare. We were preparing ourselves for a miserable Christmas. As we were getting dressed, there was a knock on the front door and I ran to see who it was. Standing there was a postman with a parcel. I thanked him and ran back with it to my Mam, who immediately opened it.

Inside there was a short letter from my Uncle Tot and Aunt Eda in Bishop Auckland. To our amazement, we also found a tin of ham, a large tin of corned beef, a wallet for me and a mirror and hairbrush for my sister, Doreen. In addition, tucked inside the letter was a £5 note. We couldn't believe our good fortune. So Dad immediately went out to buy some more food and also to get some change for the gas meter. The day was saved! But this was typical of Uncle Tot and Aunt Eda. They had no children themselves but always treated Doreen and myself as if we were their own.

By this time I was keen to be more independent and wanted to get a bicycle. So to raise the money, I managed to get a job delivering newspapers, a morning round and an evening round after school. In addition, I went around the bombed house sites searching for wood and bits of lead that I could sell as scrap to the local second-hand merchant. First I got the bicycle frame and, bit by bit, made up my pride and joy. Once it was built, I would think nothing of cycling to Brighton for the day with my mates.

However, it wasn't long before I started to think about getting a motorcycle. I managed to get hold of a pre-war model called a Calthorpe for two pounds ten shillings that had been found in a neighbour's back garden. However, after working on it for many weeks it was still decidedly beyond repair.

The time eventually arrived when I left school at 16 and started my first job as a telegraph boy at the post-office, 55 Knightsbridge. I was still living with my parents in Richbourne Terrace, Stockwell, South Lambeth in London and was busy saving up my money for my longed for motor bike. Eventually, accompanied by my father, I went along to the local Pride and Clarks to see if I could buy a motorbike on HP. Unfortunately, I faced disappointment when they said that I was not earning enough money to do this. However, my aunt and uncle, who had helped to bring me up in Bishop Auckland, heard about this. They had recently come into a little money and they very kindly sent me enough money to buy the bike outright. So, at the age of 16, I had finally achieved my ambition of buying my first motorbike, a new BSA 250, my pride and joy.

By this time, I had also met the girl who was to become my wife. Her name was Maureen and she lived in a block of flats just one road away. She used to visit a friend who lived about two houses away from where I lived and if I was outside working on my motorbike, she would stop and have a chat. However, I never asked her if she would like a ride on my pillion, as I thought it was far too dangerous. One day she stopped to tell me that her father had bought a car for her, a Morris 8. She soon started to have driving lessons and passed her test first time. I was quite impressed but not surprised as she was very intelligent and had a good job as a shorthand typist. Soon afterwards, she asked if I would like to have a ride in the car. In fact, she let me drive the car with L plates fitted and eventually taught me how to drive.

I continued to work as a telegraph boy for about one year and took telegrams to many famous people including James Stewart the film star, who I well remember gave me a sixpence tip. My wages were two pounds a week plus eight pence a week for cleaning my bike. We had to line up every day for inspection to make sure that our shoes and black leather belt were highly polished before going out on duty. About a year later, I was chosen as the smartest boy and offered the position of telegraph boy at either Buckingham Palace or the Houses of Parliament.

I picked the Houses of Parliament and was then fitted with a very smart tailored uniform that had a large embroidered badge of the Houses of Parliament on it. I was very proud of my position and worked there for about a year. In that time I got to know every bit of the House of Commons and House of Lords. While working in the House of Commons, besides taking telegrams to members, we had to keep two post offices tidy, one in the Central lobby and the other just outside the House of Commons chamber where the members used to pick up their mail. I also discovered that I had to keep the waste bins empty. At that time every member was given a copy of the New York Times, which was a very large newspaper, and most members when collecting their mail just put the newspaper straight into the waste bin. So I sorted them all out as otherwise all the waste paper was thrown into the incinerator. I used to take these newspapers to the local fish and chip shops in Kennington, where they gave me 2p a bundle which was enough to help me keep my motorbike on the road. At that time, I never dreamt that I would be back after my RAF service and attached to the Houses of Parliament, one way or another, for the next 45 years.

3 MY SERVICE IN THE RAF

I was coming up to the age of eighteen years and knew that I had to go and do my National service. I wanted to join the Navy and possibly see the world. So I went to Bedford Square in London to have my medical, which I passed A1, but was told by the Navy that I would have to sign on for seven years. This seemed far too long, consequently I went along to the RAF recruiting centre, which was about three doors away and signed on for four years.

I left home in January 1952 to go for my RAF training and got kitted out at Cardington, and then went off to West Kirby, near Liverpool, for my square bashing or basic training, which was for eight weeks. It was February and very cold when we arrived, with a lot of snow on the ground. As our arrival was very late in the day, most of the huts were already filled. So about twenty four of us were put into a hut, number 29, which had been empty for a very long time and had one small coke stove and a pile of coke, which was wet. Also a lot of the windows were missing. On my first night I lay on my bed in my formal uniform, including greatcoat, covered by the two blankets I had been issued with. After a very cold night, I eventually got to sleep for a few hours. When I woke up in the morning, I had a nice covering of snow over me, which had blown in through the missing windows! It was eight weeks of sheer hell. We did all our drill on the parade ground without gloves or greatcoat. It was so cold that if you touched the metal part of your rifle your hand stuck to it.

One particular day the drill Corporal took us onto the parade ground, where he made us stand to attention during a snowstorm. He was dressed in a greatcoat, scarf and gloves; we were wearing none of those things. One of the recruits fainted and as he fell forward the bayonet on the end of his rifle went into the leg of the man standing in front of him. We had to carry the injured man to the sickbay. When we returned to the parade ground, the drill Cpl recommenced the drill sequence again as if nothing had happened. Almost immediately a car drew up and an aircrew flight sergeant ran over to us, proceeding to give the drill Cpl a full dressing down. He told him that we should not be out in that terrible weather and in future the Cpl should dress the same way as the recruits. He warned that if it happened again, he would have him on a charge. Subsequently I developed a very bad cold, but decided not to go sick because if you did, you were put back and had to start your basic training all over again with the next intake, and then had to endure another eight weeks of hell.

The N.C.O. corporals were like little gods. Whenever our billet door was opened, and the N.C.O. Drill Corporal came in, the first man to see him would shout, "N.C.O." and everyone had to stand to attention, no matter what you were doing. Our N.C.O. used to enjoy going to the end of the billet into the room where we had washbasins and toilets, which had no doors fitted, and anyone in there had to immediately stand to attention when he approached, even if they were using the toilet. This seemed to give him great pleasure.

During my eight weeks square bashing at West Kirby, there was some very heavy flooding and many rivers burst their banks. One morning in February we were woken up very early and told to get dressed quickly and go to the parade ground. On arrival, there were a lot of military lorries waiting for us. At least two hundred recruits climbed onto the lorries, all wondering what on earth was going on. As we moved off, a sergeant on our lorry told us that we were heading for a river that had burst its banks and our job would be to fill up sandbags to try to stop the flooding. After a very long journey, we arrived at our destination, which turned out to be the River Ouse.

There seemed to be hundreds of army and air force personnel already there, with many lorries busy dropping off tons of sand. We lined up and were told to make up pairs and fill sandbags, one holding the bag open and the other filling with a shovel. We kept this up until it got dark and then went back to our lorries. After having a mug of tea and a sandwich, we tried to get some sleep.

As soon as dawn broke, we were once more out of the lorries and back filling sandbags and then stacking them along the riverbank. At about 11 o'clock, two coaches arrived, with about sixty young men, who joined us in our task. About two hours later two large vans pulled up and started serving the people from the coaches with hot meals and drinks. Then, about an hour later, they all returned to the coaches that had brought them ready to leave the area. Our sergeant went up to the coach driver, just as they were about to set off, and asked who they were. He was told they were Cambridge University students. So he went up to the coach door and shouted inside, "Thanks for your help lads," and they drove off. Meanwhile, we carried on with our task until it started to get dark. Eventually we were given a mug of tea and some sandwiches and then returned to our RAF station, arriving back in the middle of the night. We just crashed out on our beds, absolutely exhausted.

About two days later, one of the lads from our hut came in waving the newspaper and said, "You've got to see this!" The newspaper had a full page spread, praising the Cambridge University students for giving up their time and helping to put up flood barriers. We weren't very happy that we had spent two long days, working extremely hard with very little to eat, and the newspaper hadn't even bothered to give us a mention!

Eventually the day of our passing-out parade arrived and after it was over we all celebrated by having a night out at a club, which was in a large wooden building down a dark lane. To our surprise when we entered, there was a jazz band performing, which included our sadistic corporal playing his beloved trumpet. It was soon decided that it was payback time for putting us through hell over the last few weeks. So a few of the lads went outside to wait for him to leave. One of them had got hold of a large sack. When the corporal stepped out of the door into the dark lane, the sack was quickly pulled over his head and arms, thus making him drop his trumpet. This was quickly retrieved and placed on the road, where it was stamped upon by many feet. At the end of the evening, the hall emptied of people who strolled off in all directions. The corporal eventually managed to remove the sack and started looking for his trumpet. I know he didn't find it, because we heard that he went back the next day to look for it, unsuccessfully. His flattened trumpet was never found!

After a short leave, I was posted to RAF Kirkham, near Preston, where I did my training to be a turret armourer. After passing my examination, I was promoted from Aircraftsman second class (AC2) to Aircraftsman first-class (AC1).

I was then posted to RAF Marham, near King's Lynn. This was a very large base with a lot of the US Air Force stationed there. We were told they had the atomic bomb on site, so there was a lot of security. I was working on American B-29's or as we call them Washingtons, which were the same type of aeroplane that dropped the atomic bomb on Japan. Unfortunately these planes were not very reliable. I remember when I was on duty crew in December 1952 and we got a call to say that a B-29 had crashed soon after it had taken off and we had to go to the crash site to help. It was just getting light when our lorry arrived at the crash site, I will never forget the scene when we arrived. The plane had crashed, at first cutting through a line of trees and then hitting what used to be a cornfield. There were bits everywhere, but we found the tail end in one piece where the rear gunner had got out, although pretty knocked about. I believe that only the crew in the rear of the aircraft survived. We then walked over the crash site to recover any guns. I bent down to pick up a flying boot but was shocked and upset to see that it still had a foot in it. When we got to the front of the aircraft, where most of the crew would be sitting, we found that it was completely crushed flat and there was nothing more we could do. After picking up some small bits and pieces we all got back into the lorry and drove back to the camp in silence. We were told that these B-29's were being sent back to Tucson in Texas and I think at least another three of them did not make it.

I received my very first injury whilst working on a B-29 aircraft. We were bombing up one evening with 500 pound bombs, when one of the bombs that were being winched up jumped off its pulley. I had to get up and put the cable back on to the pulley. Unfortunately the bomb slipped and the cable that I was holding went up to the floor of the aircraft and trapped my hand against the floor crushing two of my fingers. Amazingly a sergeant who was standing below managed to lift the bomb, allowing me to remove my hand from the cable. I went to the sick-bay where they found I had two broken fingers.

When working on B-29s it was not unusual for the pilot to come up to you and say, "Get a parachute, you are coming up with us today." This was to make sure that whoever worked on the aircraft did their job properly because you never knew when it was your turn to go in the aircraft. This happened to me on two occasions and on the second occasion when we were coming in to land and fast approaching the runway, the co- pilot said, "Hang on. I think this is the wrong airfield. The landing beacon isn't the right one." We aborted the flight and went off to find the correct airfield. The crew all had a good laugh except me!

It was while I was stationed at RAF Marham that I bought my first car, a large Wolsey. I planned to pay for expenses by charging some of my friends a few shillings to transport them to and from the base back to their homes. I was very keen to pass my driving test and so at the first opportunity I applied for a driving test at nearby King's Lynn. About two weeks later, I was informed that the test was arranged for the following Saturday.

I reported nice and early to the test centre, where I was soon joined by the driving examiner and off we went. I was extremely careful to do things correctly as Kings Lynn had lots of narrow streets and it was always very busy on Saturdays. So I followed the driving examiner's directions very carefully until after a while we entered a very narrow street that had a very sharp right-hand bend at the end. Unfortunately, I realised I would not be able to get the car around the corner without hitting the wall. I had two or three attempts until the examiner said, "Sorry son, I've got to fail, you." I opened the driver's door and said, "Okay would you take the car round the corner for me please?" He got out, walked around the car and climbed into the driver's seat and started the car. After four attempts at negotiating the right-hand turn he said, "It's no good we will have to back out. The bend is too sharp." I got into the driver's seat again, reversed out and off we went back to the test centre. As I pulled up, the examiner looked at me and said, "Okay, you've passed!" I had that car for quite a long time but eventually sold it and went back to a motorbike as it was cheaper to run.

It was at RAF Marham, that I did my first stint at "jankers" which meant being confined to barracks when I was put on a charge with seven other men. It happened one weekend when the whole camp was shut down for seventy two hours weekend leave but eight of us were put on duty crew. In the next billet there were seven or eight American ground crew also on duty crew. At about 10 o'clock at night, the Americans decided to open up our billet door and throw in a thunder flash, which was about twice as powerful as our best firework. They then ran back to their billet laughing. Unfortunately, they picked on the wrong group, as we had one or two hard nuts amongst us, including one lad called Colin Hart. He was a very nice guy, about 6'2" tall and afraid of nothing. We let things go for about half an hour and then we burst in on the Americans and took them completely by surprise as they were playing dice and cards. Colin was first in and picked one American up and threw him through a closed window. I think two more followed.

Things were getting out of hand, when the Military Police arrived, the Americans in a large group. I suspect they came very quickly because they heard the thunder flash being let off. The American police do not take prisoners easily and gave the American airmen a bad time. But our small number of M.Ps. just took us to the guard house, put us on a charge and then returned us back to our billet as we were still on duty crew until the next day. The following morning when we came off duty crew, we were marched one at a time into our flight lieutenant, Bill Bailey's, office and given seven days confined to barracks. This meant going to the guard house at 5:30 am in full kit to be inspected by the duty officer, and then work in the cookhouse to 8 o'clock. Afterwards, we reported for normal duty, and then back again in full kit to the guard house for full inspection and worked until 10 pm, cleaning toilets or any other similar job they could find. We did our jankers willingly, as we were very grateful that our officer seemed more concerned that we had got the better of the fight with the Americans and let us off barrack room damages, which were considerable.

Soon after, I was posted to RAF Scampton, near Lincoln, where I took my exams for guns and small arms, which I passed and so became Leading Aircraftsman (L.A.C). This was where I was to meet one of my best mates for the rest of my service called Nick Nichols, who in civvy life lived in Vauxhall, about half a mile from my home. He was quite a character and I remember one day when Nick came into the billet and told me that he had been to Squadron headquarters and had seen a notice on the board, which said that the Squadron was intending to enlarge its present small band and form a marching band. Apparently, the officer in charge was keen to match the Americans, who shared the base with us and had an excellent band, and so was asking for volunteer recruits who could play the drums. Although neither of us were able to play any instrument, I pricked up my ears at this information because I knew the band were issued with fantastic uniforms, which were worn whenever they went on parade, and in addition it was usual to get Wednesday afternoons off for practice.

So the next day we decided to go and see the officer in charge. He asked if we had been in a band before. Nick said that yes, he had been in the Boys Brigade. The officer then looked at me and I just said, "Yes." Fortunately for us he didn't ask for a demonstration. Thereafter, whenever there was a Sunday parade about fourteen of us would march on to the parade ground in our magnificent uniforms, complete with a lot of gold braid and Nick and I would just go through the motions of playing, but never hitting the drums properly. Luckily for Nick and me, the rest of the lads in the band were fantastic and somehow we got away with it!

Unfortunately this didn't last for very long as a few weeks later we were both posted to RAF Upwood, Seven Squadron, near Peterborough, where I took my next exam for Bomb Armourer and passed and became a Senior Aircraftsman (S.A.C). I had always been keen to make the best of my ability and to aim for the highest promotion, and also to achieve the pay rise that went with it. For example, Nick was a national serviceman LAC, and his pay was £1 and four shillings a week while my pay as a regular S.A.C was nearly £4 and five shillings a week.

One day I was told I was going to be 'duty Armourer' over the weekend. When I arrived at the armoury, I found that I would be on my own and locked inside. As there was not much to do, I decided to have a good look around. When I went into the main office, I noticed that there were two large notice boards. At the top of one in large letters it read 'Kenya', and on the other board 'Malaya'. On each board there were the aircraft numbers and also the names of the air crew and ground crew. I looked down the list to find armourers and saw that Nick and I were down to go to Kenya. Our names were on small cards pushed into slots on the boards. As I wasn't too keen to go to Africa, I decided to swap our names over to go to Malaya. I told Nick when I next saw him and we kept our fingers crossed that nobody would find out. Soon afterwards we found out that we were off to Singapore, so job done!

The trip out there was very slow. Our first stop was in Naples to refuel and then on to Cyprus. In Cyprus, we were picked up by an RAF coach that took us to RAF Limassol, where we had a 48 hour stopover. The country at the time that we stayed there was not a very safe place, as it was during the time when EOKA was pretty active. They were even shooting British soldiers' wives when they went out shopping. A few of the lads decided to go out on our first evening and we had to have an armed soldier carrying a sten gun to accompany us when we went to a bar. We hadn't been in the bar very long when the door opened and about thirty men came in and started shouting at us to go. As there were only about ten of us decided not to argue and just left.

Soon afterwards we left Cypress and flew on to Bahrain. When we came into land late at night, it looked very desolate from the air. We were all extremely hot in the aircraft and could not wait to get out but when we jumped down onto the ground it was as hot as an oven. While the aircraft was being refuelled we were shown into a building, where there was a man pouring out lime water. But when I saw that his sweat was dripping into the glass jug, I decided not to bother! We then carried on to Delhi, and after a short stopover, onto Calcutta, where we had a two-day stay before the last hop to Singapore.

I'll never forget my stay in Calcutta as long as I live. First of all we were driven from the airport to a place that was like an old fort in the desert area. We were shown into our room on the second floor, which had openings in the walls but no windows; in fact, it was more like a cell than a room. The man who showed us to our room asked us if we would like a drink. We said, "Yes, please." But when it arrived it was a dirty yellow colour with bits floating in it. After refusing it, we asked for an unopened bottle of Schweppes tonic water. While settling into our room, I heard a lot of noise outside. I looked out of the hole in the wall of the room to see what was going on. To my amazement, I could see a dead animal of some kind being eaten by a large number of vultures. Fortunately, it was decided that the fort was not good enough for us to stay in, so we were moved to a hotel in the centre of Calcutta.

Next day we had another surprising experience in the city. We got on a bus to see the local sites and were surprised to see that it had wooden frames for windows but no glass in them and only wooden benches for seats. As we drove down the road from the hotel, the bus slowed down to go round a corner and we were amazed to see some men jump up and cling to the window frames on the outside. A very large man on the bus, who was carrying a large club, casually walked up and hit their hands so they fell off, despite the fact that the bus was travelling at about 30 mph.

We stayed in the Grand Hotel in Calcutta for two days. It was a beautiful hotel with waiters dressed in full uniform, but surprisingly enough, I think this is where a lot of us must have caught dysentery. On our first night in the hotel just before dinner, Nick and I decided to have a look outside. As we stepped out of the front door and onto the pavement, which was very wide, we were surrounded by a crowd of very small children who were begging. Nick and I were giving these children a few annas when we got into conversation with a B.O.A.C. pilot who was waiting to be picked up from our hotel. He told us that giving money to beggars was a mistake as we would be continually pestered. I then noticed a very large policeman walking past us who had started hitting a woman holding a baby with his cane for no apparent reason. I asked the pilot why he was hitting her. He said it was because she was on the pavement and as she was one of the 'unclean', she was not allowed to be there.

We went back into the hotel and after our evening meal Nick suggested that we went and had a look outside to see if the woman was still there. As we stepped out of the front door, we were absolutely amazed to see that the footpath was completely covered with people, who had put mats down and were obviously going to spend the night there. The following morning, as we left the hotel to return to our aircraft, we noticed that some men had turned on very large stopcocks in the middle of the road, which spewed out water, which then flowed down the very large gulleys that ran along the pavement. This apparently gave the people who had been there overnight the chance to have a wash and do their ablutions. Unfortunately the next day most of us were suffering with stomach trouble, which for me, turned out to be dysentery as I was to discover in due course.

Then onto our last hop, which was to be RAF Tengah, Singapore. Unfortunately, because there was so much illness, I was selected to sit in the rear of the aircraft. It was very cramped and a bumpy ride as we flew through a storm on the way down through Malaya. This didn't help as I was feeling so ill. Unfortunately, I believe some of the flying crew were suffering as well. I was in such a bad way that when we eventually arrived, I finished up being taken to the old prisoner of war camp at Changi, which was now a hospital. I stayed in hospital with dysentery for ten days before going back to join 7 Squadron at RAF Tengah.

Our time in Tengah was quite demanding. We had to 'bomb up' three or four aircraft at a time quite frequently. Most of our work was done at night and every plane was loaded with about eight 500lb bombs. Each one had to be winched up by hand. Sometimes we bombed up through the day, but it was so hot inside the aircraft that it was like an oven. So we took it in turns to winch the bombs up and as soon as the bomb you were winching clicked into place, you got out as quickly as you could. Somebody would be waiting with a bottle of Coke as soon as you jumped out.

One night a group of terrorists had climbed into our bomb dump, which was situated a couple of miles from our airfield and had stolen a large number of 500lb bombs. We were told that they had taken them into the jungle area and had actually sawn the bombs in half in order to get the explosive out! Consequently, our airfield had been put on full alert.

As armourers, because of the tremendous heat during the day, we usually worked through the night if possible and then slept during the day. Soon after the bombs had been stolen, I had just dropped off to sleep on my bed after an all night bombing-up operation, when I was woken up by an officer who said to me, "Do you realize that lying on your bed during the day is a chargeable offence?" I explained that as I was an armourer and had worked all night loading bombs onto aircraft, I was excused guard duty. He said, "Forget that. We're short of men. Everyone is on guard until further notice. The airfield is on full alert against an attack."

So that evening I reported to the headquarters building with the other airmen to be told what I would be guarding. When it got to my turn, the officer asked me what my trade was. I replied, "Armourer." He said, "Good, You can guard the bomb dump." He also told me I would have two Malayan soldiers with me. He then handed me a 303 rifle and a clip of five rounds of ammunition. I held out my hand, expecting more ammunition, but he said, "That's all you get. We can't afford to let ammunition fall into the hands of the enemy." I looked back at him and said, "But what if there are more than five". He just smiled and said, "Good luck!" As I was about to go outside, the officer came over to me and whispered, "And take care", glancing at the two Malayan soldiers who were to accompany me!

Soon afterwards, we were put into a Land Rover and driven to the bomb dump that was situated a few miles away. It consisted of a very large area surrounded by a high wire perimeter fence with a pole in the centre with a very bright light at the top. We went inside, locked the gate and walked towards the pole. Attached to it was a wind-up telephone that you could use to contact the camp, but that was quite a long way away.

I stood with my back firmly against the pole, staring into the blackness of the night, listening to the various strange noises that were coming from the thick jungle which came right up to the fence. After a while, your mind starts to play tricks on you and you start to imagine all sorts of things. It was a very long night! I tried to talk to the two Malayan soldiers but they seemed to be very uptight and nervous. Next morning, when the sun came out, I felt quite relieved as the place now seemed much more pleasant, especially when the Land Rover arrived and I was able to return to camp for my much needed sleep.

A few days later, during the night, I was woken up by my mate, John, in the next bed, who was gently calling my name. I looked across at him wondering what he wanted. In the gloom behind him I saw a movement, and then to my horror I realised it was a very large snake with its hood up. It looked like a cobra! One of the men, Taffy Williams, in the bed opposite on the other side of the room had woken up and saw what was going on. He slipped out of bed and went to the end of the room where our 'dobey-waller' slept. He was the young Indian lad who cleaned our room and did our washing. Taffy told him what was going on. The young Indian picked up a short pole with a curved blade on the end and strode down towards the snake. With one blow he removed its head. He then opened a shutter and threw the snake out onto the grass. Without any more ado, we went back to bed. Next morning, after telling our other mates what had happened we decided to go and have a look at the dangerous intruder. But to our surprise, when we got outside, all that was left were the bones and masses of ants that had stripped it clean. Nothing got wasted out there!

After a few months, we finished our tour of duty and the Squadron was sent back to RAF Upwood where we returned to our routine of bombing up planes for training. When I had a weekend pass I used to travel backwards and forwards from the base to home on my 250cc BSA motorcycle. But as I was doing a lot of long journeys I decided to buy a larger motorcycle, a Triumph 500 Speed Twin. However, my mother used to get very worried about me on my motorbike; and not without good reason. Originally there were five of us who used to go backwards and forwards to London if we had a weekend off, until one of my friends fell off his bike on an icy bend and lost three fingers on his right hand. Then a few weeks later, another mate hit a lorry head-on and was killed. So when I got home I had a chat to my mother and decided to change my motorcycle for a car at my first opportunity. I would eventually visit a big motorcycle agents called Pride and Clark at Stockwell, South London, to trade in my motorbike for a Ford 10 Prefect car, to my mother's great relief. Until that time however, if the roads were very icy, I tried not to use my motorcycle, but got a travel warrant to go home by train instead.

We would leave the camp on Friday after work and return on the Sunday night. We had to be back in camp by seven o'clock Monday morning. If you were late back, you would be on a charge. I remember one particular weekend when Nick and I caught the late train back on a Sunday night. It stopped at most stations and I think it was the milk train. It was a very cold night, and the train had very old carriages which seemed to have no heating. We both stretched out on a seat and dropped off to sleep. It was much later when I was woken up by a lot of noise. I think somebody had knocked over some milk churns. I looked out of our carriage window to see what was going on and then to my horror I saw the name of the station and realised we had passed the station where we were meant to get off. I quickly woke up Nick and we both jumped down onto the platform, wondering how on earth we were going to get to our camp, which was quite a long way off. At this point, I noticed a train standing on the opposite track facing the other way. I could hear the doors banging and realised it was getting ready to leave. My spirits sank as I knew that if we had to run along the platform to the end in order to cross over the track, we would miss the train. So there was only one thing for it. We jumped down underneath the train between the carriages and quickly crossed over the lines. Opening the first carriage door, we climbed in and sat down with some relief just as the train pulled away.

About twenty minutes later we pulled up at our correct station, but unfortunately the coach that used to meet us there and take us to our camp had already left. However, once more we were in luck. A van was passing by and the driver shouted down, "Have you lads missed your coach?" I replied that yes, we had and he said, "Jump in the van, I'm going past your camp." With great relief we climbed into the van and soon arrived at our camp with about ten minutes to spare. As we booked into the guard room, the sergeant said, "You were certainly cutting it a bit fine, weren't you?" So from then on we decided it was probably more prudent to catch an early train. I continued to serve at

RAF Upwood until I was demobbed. But I was told that I would still be on reserve for the next two years.

DRIVEN TO DOWNING STREET

Aged 4 at Etherley, County Durham, 1938

Aged 5 at Purley

Aged 14 with sister Doreen aged 7

Aged 16 in London, 1949

Inside Lincoln, winching up a bomb   With fellow armourers "bombing up"

Newspaper report of bomb compound attack, RAF Tengah, 1954

With Nick and Browning machine gun　　**Waiting to load the bombs**

**With Mike Marshall Ride (far left) & Nick Nichols (5th left).
Party for end of tour in Singapore.**

4 LIFE AFTER THE RAF

By now Mam and Dad had moved to a council flat in Kennington, not far from the Oval cricket ground. We lived in flat 47 Dolland House and our next-door neighbour had a daughter, Rose, whose boyfriend was called Buster Edwards, who seemed to stay there most of the time. He was later to become one of the infamous 'Great Train Robbers'. I remember one particular day, when there was a knock on the door and Buster handed my father a large suitcase and said, "Hang on to this lot, it's full of watches. The police are after me," before running off. My father went straight over to the other side of the flat (we were on the second floor), opened the window and threw the suitcase out. Dad was pretty tough and wouldn't be pushed around by anybody. He certainly would never allow himself to be involved in anything illegal even if it did mean upsetting an obviously 'dodgy' character like Buster.

After a short leave, I decided to return to my job at the post office as my seniority counted whilst I was in the RAF. So I went as a sorter/ postman at the London Victoria Post Office. I used to cycle to work, as I had to start my shift at 5.30 in the morning and there were very few buses. Usually, I could get to the sorting office in about fifteen minutes. Since there were no parking restrictions at this time, I just left my bicycle outside the front entrance.

When it came time for my first holiday, I asked my friend Harry Featherstone if he fancied a trip to France. It was a bit ambitious, as we were aiming to go to Paris and back in one week, however off we went. When we arrived at Dover port, there was a very bad storm and no one was allowed onto the ferry. The ferries at that time were much smaller than today. So, we found a bus shelter close to the docks and spent the night in that. At first light it had stopped raining but was very windy. When we went back into the ferry office, we were told that they were letting people on but were not sure when we would leave, although it would be as soon as the wind dropped.

Once on board, we discovered that it was quite full of American soldiers. We decided to go downstairs to the washrooms, but that was a big mistake as all the toilets were full up with Americans being seasick, and we were still tied up to the dock! To give an idea of how rough it actually was, when we filled up the wash basin with water, the roll of the ship immediately emptied the basin. I said to my friend Harry, "Let's go up onto the top deck get into the fresh air." As we climbed the stairs, we could hear glasses and crockery smashing. Once on deck we ran into one of the crew who said, "Look lads, my advice is to put your backs to the walls and look at the horizon." Eventually the wind dropped quite a bit and we set sail for Calais.

Unfortunately, the ferry was still rolling quite a lot as there were no stabilisers on them at that time. As we approached Calais, we had more bad news when we were told that we couldn't go into port as the captain of the French ferry that was already there had said it was too rough for him to come out. In fact, it took about another three hours before we finally went in and docked.

When we eventually disembarked from the ferry, it felt to me as though the dock was moving up and down. Anyway the wind had dropped, the sun had come out and our first aim was to get to Arras. However, this was not an easy trip as the roads were in a terrible state. Quite often, we found places where bombs had been dropped and the road was impassable, so we had to drive off into the fields to get round them. In some of the villages we passed, we could see where a battle had taken place with bullet holes everywhere. We finally arrived in Arras and, needing to find somewhere to get a night's sleep, we looked around and came across a house where the owner let us have a room.

The next morning Harry and I had a chat and decided that we couldn't make Paris in the time remaining and, as we were running out of money, we should reluctantly start back to Calais. After a few hours on the road it soon became clear that we had another problem, as I now needed oil for my motorbike. Eventually we came to a village where we found oil and petrol for sale. I asked the old lady in charge, if we could do a deal for oil in exchange for a packet of tea I had with me, as I was short of money with just enough left to get me home. She spoke a little English and said, "Is it Liptons?" I took a packet out of my saddlebag and said that no it was something else, but she seemed happy enough. So I was able to put a little more oil in the tank, at least enough to get us to Calais, although by this time we had also run out of food.

Once on the ferry, we went along to the Purser's office to change our few French francs into English money. When we got to the front of the queue, I put a bag of coins onto the table. The officer took one look at this and said, "We don't change coins, only notes." I said, "But we have to get back to London and we need money for a meal and petrol." He just said, "Sorry."

I was then tapped on the shoulder by the person standing behind me. When I looked around I saw a well-dressed middle aged man, who said, "Here you are, take this", and handed me a one pound note. I thanked him and offered him my bag of coins. He said, "No, you keep them." I waited for him to come out of the Purser's office and went over to him and said that I'd like to thank him again and could I have his address to repay him later. He again refused and said, "It's okay, glad to have been of help." As he glanced at my jacket, I realised I was wearing my RAF tunic top and thought that was probably the reason for his kindness. As soon as we disembarked at the ferry port, Harry and I bought some fish and chips, topped up the petrol and still had change from our pound note as we made our way home to London.

I continued with my job at the post office. However I decided after a few months that this was not the right life for me. I had to start work at 5.30 am; sort letters, then deliver them and then walk back to the Victoria sorting office and do a second delivery (which was nearly all blocks of flats). In addition, I found it was boring and without challenges after my interesting life in the RAF. So I decided there was no way I was going to do this for the rest of my life, although I wasn't quite sure what I wanted to do. However, two of my uncles who had been Sergeants in the Police Force often suggested that I should join the police and since I had always been quite interested in the idea, I decided to give it a go.

I sent off for an application form, filled it in and posted it off. Soon afterwards I received an invitation to sit the written entrance examination, which I did and then about a week later I was asked to report for an interview. When I arrived, I found there were about 25 other young men waiting with me for their interviews. We were told to undress and just stand in our underpants before being called in, one at a time, to stand in front of four high ranking officers to answer various questions. After the interview, we were told to get dressed and wait. Soon afterwards an officer came in with a clipboard to tell us who had passed and I was pleased to hear that I was one of them.

About two weeks later I received a letter telling me to report to Hendon Police College. On arrival I received my uniform and started the eight week training course. I enjoyed it all very much but my favourite part was the P.E. which included long distance runs. These always finished back at Hendon where you ran through the gates to the swimming pool, dived in and swam a length of the pool before racing to the showers and back into your uniform. I was always in the first two or three to finish because when I was in the RAF, I was a member of their cross country team and it was very much my favourite sport.

About a week before we were due to finish the training, my intake was called into the officer in charge's office, one at a time, to be told where we were going to be posted to. When my turn came, he told me that I was going to be put into a section house in East London. Now this happened to have been one of the two section houses I had already been sent to see during training and I had not been very impressed to say the least. The rooms were very small, about 10ft by 5ft, with a small bed and a locker and the shower and toilet were about 50 yards away. However, the worst bit was that you were charged so much for your room that it took most of your wages!

I explained to the officer that I had been hoping to be based in Central London, an area I knew well from my Post Office days. In addition, I wanted to live with my parents for a while, if possible, as I had been away from home for nearly four years in the RAF and I was hoping to help towards their outgoings. He looked at me and said, "What are you a mammy's boy?" I bit my lip as his stupid remark infuriated me but nevertheless I continued calmly, "I do have one request. In a couple of week's time on the Saturday I've been asked to be best man at my sister's wedding and to drive the wedding car. I wonder if I could have the day off then?" I hadn't had a single day's leave during the previous few weeks and thought the request was very reasonable. However, the officer glanced at a list in front of him and said. "No, we can't give you any time off then. You won't be able to go." This was the final straw. I paused for a moment before saying, "Yes, I will. You can have my resignation now." He looked aghast and said, "Do you know how much your training has cost?" However, my mind was made up. He could tell from my attitude that I was serious, so he took out a form of resignation which I signed and I walked out of his office. After packing my bags, I walked out of Hendon and made my way back to London.

On leaving the railway station I saw a newspaper vendor in the street and I bought a copy of the Evening Standard from him, looked in the jobs section and saw an advert, 'driver wanted'. I rang them up and they told me they were 'The National Fur Company' in Knightsbridge. I went straight along for an interview and was told that the job would be to pick up fur coats for cleaning and storage. The man in charge was ex-military and said it was a very responsible job. However, I must have made a good impression as he gave me the job straight away. I enjoyed the work very much and stayed there for several months. While I was there I met the other driver, Denis Oliver, who had also been in the RAF. He was to become a lifelong friend. Little did I know then that our destinies would to be linked to lead us along a similar exciting path for many years into the future.

One day when I was out in the van and passing what was then the door of the Treasury which overlooked St James's Park, I saw my father, who was a security guard, standing in the doorway. I stopped and he invited me in to have a cup of tea. We went into a small room, just inside the front door. This action changed the rest of my life, as there was also a man in the room called Charlie Pierce. He was a government driver, who drove the Treasury minister. We had a long chat and he said to me. "Why are you wasting your time in that job? Why don't you apply for a job with us at the GCS?" This was the Government Car Service and apparently they were looking for more drivers, but only wanted ex-service personnel. As I fitted the bill, he gave me the telephone number of the Superintendent in charge, who I telephoned the next day for an interview. A week later I went for the interview and was told I could start, although only as a night driver so that I could get to know all the government buildings in the London area. Little did I know that I would be working there for the next 47 years leading an extremely exciting life!

5 EARLY YEARS IN THE GOVERNMENT CAR SERVICE (GCS) "POOL"

At the age of 22, stepping into the GCS depot at Kingston House Garage in Kensington felt much like being back in the RAF. In those days, the Government Car Service only accepted ex-military men, who were much older than myself, and ran it with military precision and discipline. Four of these drivers had been prisoners of war during the Second World War, two captured by the Germans and two by the Japanese. Perhaps not surprisingly, the two who had been in the Japanese prisoner of war camps refused to drive anyone who was Japanese. One of the other two drivers who had been captured by the Germans was called Frankie Hall, who had been at Dunkirk in a tank. One day when I was chatting to him, he told me how he had been captured. He explained that his orders were to hold back the Germans who were advancing towards them. He said that one day he was looking through the tank telescope when he heard some knocking on the top hatch. Thinking it was an officer with some new orders, he opened the hatch, only to see a German officer, who said, "Okay, for you, the war is over!" However it was far from over, as he was then made to walk with the rest of the prisoners to a prison camp in Poland. Fortunately, he seemed to have recovered from his experience and we became great friends.

In the GCS, just like in the services, discipline was strict. At the slightest hint of an unwashed or unclean shirt, the bosses would send you home without pay. When you went into the garage in order to start your day's work, you had to clock on at the latest eight o'clock. If the time on the clock was a minute before eight o'clock, your clock card would be in the black. But as soon as it passed eight o'clock, it showed red. Any driver with more than two reds in a week was taken into the office and warned to get in on time or be out of a job.

In addition, if you were seen outside the depot not wearing your hat while on duty, it could lead to suspension. Drivers were also expected to clean and vacuum their cars every night before clocking off, even at 1am. So the workforce had to be pretty tough. Not that everyone, however, had a moustache above a stiff upper lip: around half of the three hundred drivers were women. These ladies had originally been recruited to drive members of the War Cabinet through London's bomb-stricken streets during World War II. It was their bravery that led to the inception of the Government Car Service.

As a night driver there was quite a lot of driving to be done. One of my main jobs was to pick up a Superintendent who travelled around all the government and official buildings. He would just turn up at any time throughout the night, in order to make sure that the security man was awake and doing his rounds of the building. The good side of this for me was that I got to know most of London and the suburbs.

After working for about six months, I was told there was a vacancy to work on days as a pool driver, which suited me even better. I was quite excited and pleased to take the job as this was considered the next step on the ladder towards getting a more prestigious position as an allocated driver with a minister. At that time, the GCS did all kinds of varied, interesting and exciting government driving jobs, including picking up for the government Central Office of Information any guests who were visiting London and to look after them during their stay. So I was able to start doing quite a lot of these varied jobs and was enjoying the life immensely.

I had so many interesting passengers, but one man stood out. I remember picking him up from London airport and taking him to the

Home Office. I was driving him for about a week during which time we visited one or two prisons. It was on the second day that he told me that he was the Government Hangman for Overseas Protectorates. I was quite surprised to hear this and more than a little interested. I asked him if he had hanged many people. He said that yes, quite a lot of terrorists, and once or twice he had hanged as many as eight people in a day. I asked him how he felt about doing the job and it was then that he told me about some of the terrible things these terrorists had done. There was one case in North Africa, where a large group of British soldiers had been invited to a wedding celebration. When they were all seated in the hall, the doors were shut and a bomb exploded which killed and badly injured a large number of them. He obviously felt that knowing about such atrocities had made his job easier.

One day, the Superintendent said he had been very pleased with my work and that there was now a vacancy for another driver. He wondered if I had any other ex-service friends who would be interested in taking a job. I recommended Denis Oliver who had been with me at the National Fur Company and was also ex- RAF He was delighted when I mentioned the job to him, and I was pleased when he started with the GCS, because there were now two 'young lads', as the other drivers liked to call us. Like me, Denis had to start the hard way as a night driver.

A short time later, Denis came up to me and asked if I would do him a big favour and go back on nights so that he could go onto days as he was getting married and it would be much more convenient. I was a bit reluctant at first, but agreed, saying he owed me one big favour. Anyway, about three months later I was asked to go back on days as well. I am now very pleased that I was able to help Denis out as we have been close friends for over forty years. He was later to become Margaret Thatcher's official driver for many years, so he had good reason to be pleased that I had recommended him originally for a position in the GCS.

My next aim in the job was to get a permanent allocation to a minister, because you were then able to get into a regular routine with your life. This was much harder to achieve because there were about 150 non-allocated, or "pool" drivers but only about 30 allocated drivers. So vacancies were very few.

While continuing to work in "the pool", I did many different assignments, but one particular job that sticks in my mind was when I had to pick up three high-ranking RAF officers in full uniform from the Air Ministry and take them to Shoeburyness, which at that time was where they tested new weapons and explosives. We left London and drove down the A13, which was a dual carriageway. After about 5 miles we went onto a roundabout and the officer next to me pointed out that there was a police car in the lay-by. We continued on our journey and had travelled about half a mile when the officer said, "That police car is coming up behind us very fast and it's got its headlights full on." As it got closer to us, the police car started to flash its headlights. As there was no speed limit in those days on the main roads, the officer said to me, "We haven't done anything wrong so let's give them a run for their money!"

At that time I was driving a large Wolsey car. In fact, it was the same model that the police had behind us. I put my foot hard down on the accelerator and our car started to pull away from the police car. My three passengers were getting quite excited and enjoying the ride. However, I was starting to get a bit worried but the officer sitting next to me, who was a Group Captain said, "Don't worry, you're just following orders."

Many miles later, as we approached Shoeburyness the officer said, "I can see there's a lay-by up ahead, just pull in and stop." This we did, quickly followed by the police car. The police officer came up to our car and said, "Alright, get out of the car." As I did so my three passengers also got out. On seeing this array of uniforms, the police officer's attitude changed immediately and he looked a little sheepish.

The Group Captain said, "Why have you stopped us? We've done nothing wrong." The police officer then proceeded to explain that as we came round the roundabout, he'd noticed that we had no tax. The Group Captain then said angrily, "You mean to tell us that you chased us for about 15 miles because of a tax disc? Well for your information, this is an official government car, which is exempt from tax. We didn't stop because it would have been very dangerous to stop on that narrow dual carriageway." He then turned to me and said, "Driver, get back in the car or we'll be late." A little while later when we arrived at Shoeburyness depot, the group captain said to me, "Park the car and come and join us for a cup of tea and something to eat. You've earned it."

Whilst we were having our tea, I got chatting to one of the officers and asked the reason why we were at the testing ground. He told me that they were there to re-enact an accident that had killed an RAF Sergeant a couple of years before. As he started to recount the incident, I suddenly realised with astonishment that he was talking about the sergeant I had served with a few years before, who had been killed.

I explained to him that I had been in the RAF serving as an S.A.C. Armourer and had actually loaded bombs onto Lincoln aircraft with that self same sergeant many times. I cannot remember where I was when I heard about the incident of my Sergeant being killed, but I do remember being told that the sergeant and another airman were in a tractor that was pulling bomb-trolleys loaded with bombs towards an aircraft when one of the bombs went off. Both the tractor driver and the Sergeant were blown off the tractor by the blast and I understand that they were rushed to hospital. The sergeant's wife who lived in married quarters was immediately taken to his bedside but was relieved to see him sitting up in bed and talking. But unfortunately, a short time, later he just closed his eyes and his head dropped forward. They thought he had gone to sleep but a doctor in the ward came to his bedside and said that he was very sorry but he had died. Apparently it was secondary shock.

The Group Captain turned to me and continued his conversation saying that they could not understand why the bomb had gone off and were going to set up a test situation. I asked if I could see the test and he agreed. After many experiments, they reached the conclusion that as the bombs were just sitting on cradles and not strapped down and the trolleys had been pulled over the rough ground towards the aircraft, the bombs were inclined to bounce around. The bomb that went off must have twisted until the fuse in its nose came in contact with the rubber wheels on the trolley, which became very hot and caused the explosion.

After the test was finished and we were about to leave, an army officer came up to the group captain and said, "Excuse me, I know you are ready to leave, but we're just about to test a new armour piercing shell. Would you like to see the demonstration?" I was pleased to hear them answer yes as I thought it would be very interesting. So we were then taken into a large steel bunker with walls of about 3 inch thick steel. They had cut very thin slits into the steel through which, if you got up close to them, you could see in the distance about 500 yards away, a large crane holding up a large steel plate of armour. Next to us there was a tank, waiting to fire.

Once we were all settled into the bunker, a siren sounded to let people know that the gun was about to fire. Everyone else on this site took cover in bunkers and we had a ten second countdown. Most of the men in our bunker were looking through the slits at the armour plating ready to watch the shell hit. The countdown started and on the shout of 10, the tank fired its shell. The blast was unbelievable and followed by a very loud bang. Peering through a slit, I could see that there was now a large hole in the steel plate. There was a lot of cheering and shouting when we suddenly noticed that one of the officers I had brought down with us was screaming and holding his hand over his left eye. Apparently, a small splinter of steel had blasted back from the target and come through the slit into his eye. He was in great pain, so the officer in charge said we needed to get him back to London as quickly as possible. We got him back into my car and drove straight to Moorfields Eye Hospital, where they were waiting for him. A few days later, the Car

Service Superintendent called me into the office to say that he had a message to let me know that thankfully the officer's eye had been saved.

One of the best things about being in the GCS 'pool' was that you got to meet quite a lot of important people and did some very interesting jobs. I remember one occasion when I was given the task of picking up a very high ranking RAF officer at Stansted airfield. In those days it was quite a small airfield, and I think the RAF was also stationed there. My job was to take him to the Air Ministry in the Whitehall area. His plane landed at about midday, so it was decided to have lunch before leaving for London.

Unfortunately, and without warning, we had one of the dreaded 'smogs', which came down on us. Luckily we don't seem to get them any more, as there is far less smoke around to mix in with any fog, since there are hardly any coal fires and air pollution generally has been reduced. There used to be a saying that you couldn't see a hand in front of your face, and that was absolutely true on this occasion.

The officer said, "It's getting bad, so I think we'd better get started." As we set off, the smog was very patchy. It would be clear for about 100 yards and then became worse. We were hoping it might clear as we went along, but after about 10 miles the smog was getting extremely thick. In fact, I couldn't even see the end of the car's bonnet. Fortunately I had a torch in the car, so the officer got out and walked in front of the car, shining the light on the ground to show the way, although we still had to travel very slowly as there were abandoned cars all along the roads. In addition, I had to open the driver's door and peer out so that I could just about make out the white line in the middle of the road and use this as a guide, whilst also keeping an eye on the torchlight. Every now and then there would be a clear patch for a short distance and the officer would jump back in the car until the next thick patch arose.

Eventually we reached North London and found ourselves on the ring road around Regents Park. However, we were not sure which was the exit leading South. I got out of the car to look for a road sign and, after finding one, I turned to go back to the car only to discover that the smog had turned so very thick that I couldn't find it! It was a bit like putting on a blindfold and turning around two or three times. You lose all sense of direction in smog. Not only can you not see but you cannot hear properly either, as everything sounds muffled. As I walked along close to the park railings, I started to shout out and after a few minutes was relieved to hear a cry of, "Over here," from my officer.

Once we got into Baker Street, which had all the street lights on, we made better progress and I was eventually able to get the officer safely to the Air Ministry. I didn't get home that night because I was so absolutely exhausted that I slept in the car. Later I discovered that the officer had been very kind and had sent an extremely complimentary letter to my Superintendent praising my driving skills and endeavour.

6 GAINING EXPERIENCE

I was about three to four years in the "pool" but on occasions when a minister's allocated driver went sick or on holiday, I might get the chance to stand in for them. During these years, I met and drove many famous people and had many unforgettable experiences. One of the jobs was the weekly or monthly cashier run. I would have to take a Humber Pullman, which was a very large car with a glass partition also used by ministers, up to the City of London. At a bank next to the Bank of England, I would pick up three cashiers and the guard, who was usually a retired police officer. They would get into the car with a very large bag, which was full of cash. On the monthly run, we carried about £90,000. When you think that my wage was about £8-£9 a week, £90,000 was a lot of cash! The bag had a chain attached to it, which went through a ring in the floor of the car and then attached to the cashier's wrist. The guard had a truncheon, usually hidden up his sleeve, and off we went to government buildings often outside London to do the monthly payout, which was always in cash.

This went on for a long time, until one day, one of the cars was stopped and attacked and the cash was taken. The lady driver was sprayed in the face with some kind of chemical and was in a bad way for a long time. Soon after this they stopped paying by cash and started to open bank accounts for all civil servants.

Another job I was given, while I was in the pool was to go out to a Fighter Headquarters outside London to pick up a German high ranking officer (I believe his name was Colonel von Choltitz). I was informed by one of the police motorcycle escorts that he thought he was the general who had been told to burn Paris by Hitler as the Allies approached, but he had refused. I was told to take him to the London Guildhall, where he was to receive an honour for his bravery in refusing to burn Paris. They gave me a brand-new Austin Princess limousine for the job and when I arrived at the RAF Headquarters I was met by two police motorcycle outriders to act as an escort.

The German officer came out of the front door with a very high ranking British RAF officer at his side. We were quite taken aback as he was wearing his full German general's uniform and looked fantastic. I put him in the car and we were ready to set off to the city of London. Just as we were on the point of leaving, one of the motorcycle escorts told me to be prepared, as they had heard there might be a bit of trouble when we got to the Guildhall. Apparently, they were expecting some protesters. This was the understatement of the week, because as I turned into the street leading to the Guildhall entrance there seemed to be hundreds of protesters.

One of the police motorcyclists drove up to my car window and said, "Whatever you do, don't stop". As I was travelling quite fast, the crowd parted and I went straight through. Unfortunately, the mob was well prepared with bricks, sticks and other things which they started throwing at us. When I arrived at the door of the main entrance inside the courtyard of the Guildhall I pulled up, got out and opened the passenger door. The German officer stepped down and smiled as though it was all in a day's work. One of the police motorcyclists came up to me and said, "Well done, but we've got to go back the same way later on". Unfortunately, by this time, my car was in a bad way and covered in paint and dents. Luckily no windows were broken.

After the ceremony was finished, the officer came out of the door and got back into my car. By this time, more police had arrived and the demonstrators were far fewer. Consequently, we got away with very little resistance and continued back to Fighter Headquarters. I pulled up and opened the door, and the general stepped out. He walked up to me and the police escort, shook our hands and said, "Thank you, a job very well done."

Another very memorable assignment I had in the car pool in July 1959 was to pick up Lord Brabazon, who I was told was the first Englishman to hold a pilot's licence, and to take him from London to Hyde airport on the south coast. Here we were to meet up with Mme Bleriot, the wife of Louis Bleriot, the first man to fly over the English Channel before he crash-landed on the cliffs near Dover. I was to take them to the exact spot of this historic event, where a ceremony was to be held to commemorate the anniversary of his landing. After the ceremony, Lord Brabazon had to go directly back to London. So the government car service had provided another car to take Mme Bleriot back to Hyde airport to fly back to France.

After the service, we left the Dover Memorial site and were driving along a narrow road behind Mme Bleriot's car, when suddenly her car went over onto its side as one of the back wheels had come off. The wheel disappeared through a hedge and didn't stop until it hit a house wall. We immediately stopped and ran over to her car and opened the back passenger door, not knowing what to expect. Fortunately, when Mme Bleriot was helped out of the car she seemed none the worse for her ordeal. She straightened her hat, climbed into our car and off we went to Hyde airport. As the plane took off, we waved goodbye, much to our relief. Later Lord Brabazon checked on her well-being and learnt that she was fine.

As a pool driver you could be asked to stand in if an allocated driver went sick or was on leave and we had the opportunity to drive their Minister while they were away. I drove a number of ministers during this period in the pool, but the one I will always particularly remember is Lord Hailsham. He lived in a house near Wimbledon Common. One Friday morning I was told by the Government Car Service

Superintendent that Lord Hailsham's regular driver was on holiday for two weeks, so I would be driving him from Monday. So, on the Monday morning I drove to his home, knocked on the door and introduced myself. I explained that I had been allocated as his driver for the next two weeks, to replace his usual driver who was on holiday. He asked my name and said, "Oh, alright, I'll be out in about ten minutes".

As he came out I saw to my surprise that he was carrying not only his red box, but also a fold-up bicycle. He gave me the red box and said, "Put that the car". He then bent down and put on his bicycle clips, unfolded his bicycle, placed his bowler hat on his head and jumped onto his bicycle. I believe it was called a Moulton, one of those that folds up and has very small wheels. He then turned to me and said, "I'll race you to my office in Whitehall". The office was in Richmond Terrace, which is no longer there, but was on the other side of Whitehall to Downing Street. I held back and made sure that he was always in front of me for security reasons. It was quite a long way from Wimbledon to Whitehall, as he dived in and out of the traffic.

When he arrived, I saw him jump off the bike and walk up to the doorway where he stood waiting for me. I pulled up outside his office and took out the red box and handed it to him. He said, "There you are. I knew I'd beat you." But little did he know that I'd already decided that it was best to let him win and had no intention of arriving without him!

Another minister I drove was Lennox Boyd, who was Secretary of State for the Colonies who also had protection from Special Branch. He lived in Belgravia, which was quite close to Buckingham Palace, and his office was in Church House in Westminster. His driver had gone sick and I had to stand in for him. So I went to his home to pick him up, rang the doorbell and the door was answered by his butler who asked me to come in as Lennox Boyd wanted to speak to me. I went through into his sitting room. He asked me to sit down and then had a chat with me, as he wanted to know about my previous jobs and life and experiences in the GCS. He also asked if I would be willing to work at weekends as his permanent driver didn't like working weekends. I told him that as I was saving up to try and buy a house I would work any day or any weekend that he wanted. He then asked me what kind of car I had outside to drive him in. I said it was a Humber Pullman limousine. He then opened a drawer, took out a bunch of keys and handed them to me. He told me to go round to the mews at the back of his house, take his car out of the garage, leave my Humber in the garage and bring his car round to the front door. To my surprise, when I opened the garage door, I found a Rolls-Royce convertible. I jumped in with great excitement, as I had never driven a Rolls-Royce in my life before and took it round to the front door, where I was met by Lennox Boyd's protection officer, whose name was Sergeant Wren. The sergeant and I had a little chat as we made our introductions and, after a while, we were to become good friends and I was to work with him on many occasions.

The Minister came out of the front door and said that he wanted the hood down on the car. He made the protection officer sit in the back seat whilst he jumped into the front seat next to me. Then off we went to his office at Church House near Whitehall. Whilst we were there, the car was just left outside the front door with the top-down. I asked Sgt Wren, if he was armed and he took out a small handgun from his coat pocket, showed it to me and said, "Yes, this is it." Very reassuring and how things have changed!

Lennox Boyd was a very kind and considerate gentleman. I remember that one of the things he liked to do when we were travelling in London was to stop off at a shop to buy the 'Evening Standard'. When he got back in the car, he had always bought the Special Branch officer and myself a bar of chocolate. Not many Ministers at that time would have been so thoughtful! About two weeks later, Lennox Boyd got in touch with me and asked if I would work for him privately the next weekend, as it was an unofficial trip. I happily agreed and he explained to me that it was to travel to an important Lady's house just outside Dover, where they were having a house party. He would be staying there for the weekend, so he would book me into a hotel in Dover. I think it was called the 'Seven Clouds' hotel.

I picked him up from his London house very early on Saturday morning and drove down to Dover, dropped him off at the house where he was staying and continued to the hotel that he had booked me into. He had already told me that he would telephone me if he needed me. In fact, I had only been there for a couple of hours when he telephoned to say that he wanted to see me as soon as I could possibly get back to him.

On arrival, I was asked into the sitting room and was surprised to be told that the cook had run off with the butler! As they were due to have a dinner party for ten people, he asked if I would be willing to help and act as the butler for the evening. The lady of the house would do the cooking. I explained to him that I'd never served at table before and as ten people would be dining it would be rather a daunting experience. He smiled and shrugged and said, "Just do your best. I'm sure you will manage."

To my great relief, all went very well and the lady of the house said, "Thank you very much, you did extremely well." The minister gave me a £10 tip for the extra work and effort I'd put in over the weekend, as well as the £10 wages for the weekend's driving. My pay at that time in the Government Car Service was only just over £8 a week basic pay. A couple of weeks later he got in touch with me again and asked me if I would be willing to work for him privately over the next weekend. I said I would be pleased to do this and on the Saturday morning my father drove me over to Lennox Boyd's house. As I got out of the car, I said to my Dad, "Could you wait outside until I find out how long I will be needed?" He could then arrange a pick-up time to collect me.

I rang the doorbell and the butler opened the door asking me to come in as Mr Lennox Boyd wanted a word with me. I entered his sitting room, and he said to me that he was very sorry, but his trip had unfortunately been called off at the last minute. He explained that he wouldn't need me now but handed me ten pounds for my trouble. Just imagine my delight as this was more than my weekly salary. Unfortunately, when his regular driver got wind of the fact that I was working weekends for him and getting good tips, he accused me of trying to steal his minister!

Little did he know that Lennox Boyd had in fact asked me to drive him regularly and I had refused, because I had to explain to him that ministerial driving jobs were allocated strictly on seniority.

Shortly afterwards, when I was standing in again for his driver (as Lennox Boyd used to ask for me whenever his driver was off sick) we were out driving along Piccadilly towards Piccadilly Circus. As I stopped at the pedestrian crossing just past the Ritz hotel, the Minister said, "Hello" to a man waiting to cross the road and asked if he could give him a lift. It was only then that I realised that it was David Niven, the film star. He jumped in the car, and we dropped him off just near Leicester Square.

Our journeys were always quite unpredictable. Another time, we picked up a man in the Strand, who Lennox Boyd introduced to me as the Duke of Northumberland. After a few minutes conversation they had a bit of a laugh as he said to the Duke that he had one of his relatives driving him. He said to the Duke, "This is Mr Smithson and, as you know, the Northumberlands have the name Smithson in their family history." He also explained that my family originally came from Northumberland. The Duke seemed quite interested and we all had a good laugh.

It was quite soon after this that Lennox Boyd was elevated to the peerage and became Viscount Boyd of Merton. I met him several times over the next few years, and he always stopped and had a word with me. I was very sorry to be told one day that he'd been knocked down and killed by a taxi in The Kings Road in Chelsea, as he was crossing the road to look in a shop window that was selling antique walking sticks. I understand that he was a great collector of walking sticks, as he had a large collection at home.

I drove quite a few cabinet ministers over the next year or so, as whenever a driver went sick or on holiday, I was asked to stand in for them. These included Lord Butler, Home Secretary, Ted Heath, Harold Macmillan, Selwyn Lloyd, and Sir Alec Douglas Home. I must say it was a pleasure as generally they were all very nice people to work for. Sir Alec

Douglas Home was an exceptionally, very nice man. One day, I remember I had to collect him to take to a Privy Council meeting with the Queen at Goodwood House. I picked him up at his residence in Chelsea and was told that Lady Home had made up a picnic hamper for us to share on the way to Goodwood House. As it was a lovely day, we chose a good spot to park up at the side of the road and shared the picnic, whilst having a very relaxed chat, which I will always remember. I thought he was a true gentleman, as he always seemed to treat me as an equal. But this wasn't the case with all ministers, for example, when I drove Selwyn Lloyd, the Foreign Secretary, at the time of the Suez crisis. I knew that he wasn't the easiest person to get on with, as he had the habit of not talking directly to the driver, but would ask either his secretary or his Special Branch man to tell the driver what to do. For example, he would ask the protection officer to tell me to stop at the next traffic lights. The officer would then say, "Stop at the lights", as though I hadn't heard. I felt as though he thought it was beneath him to speak to me. But I believe he was an ex-high-ranking guard's officer of the old school, which explained a lot.

This all came to a head on one particular day when I had to take him to a Cabinet meeting at No.10, where they were deciding whether to go to war over Suez. After a considerable amount of time, all the Cabinet ministers left except the Foreign Secretary. There were very large crowds waiting for his appearance to see if we were going to go to war over Suez. After a while he emerged and stood on the step of number 10. The crowd cheered him as he walked towards the official car. Selwyn Lloyd stood and waved at the crowd with dignity and gravitas. He stepped into my car, and his Special Branch man got in and sat next to me. Then like most cars, the Humber Pullman chose her moment to reveal her worst fault. I turned the key and pushed the starter button. Silence. The battery had died without warning. Instead of a minister gliding towards Whitehall dispensing reassuring waves, the car refused to start. Selwyn Lloyd kept saying, "Drive on, drive on!" With a sinking heart, I turned to the protection officer and said, "You will have to get out and give me a push." Giving me an old-fashioned look, he jumped out and went over to the policeman on duty at the door of Number 10 said, "Quick, give us a push", which he did. At this moment, the crowd in Downing Street went very quiet. Luckily, the car started very quickly and we were off on our way through cheering crowds to the House of Commons. Fortunately, no one took a photograph. It certainly wouldn't have looked very good on the front page of a newspaper to see the Foreign Secretary announcing. "We are going to war," with a photo of him being pushed down Downing Street in his car! Nevertheless the Foreign Secretary was so angry; he smashed the interior clock with his walking stick and shouted, "I never want to see this car again!"

Apparently this had happened more than once with other GCS cars but after this embarrassing moment, the Government Car Service decided that no minister's car would be allowed to leave the depot on official business without a spare battery being fitted. This rule would last for a number of years with all ministerial cars until they became more reliable.

The car of choice at that time for all Cabinet ministers was the Humber Pullman, although later they were changed to Austin Princess limousines. Many of the women drivers hated the car because of its heavy steering. The cars we drove had non-adjustable front seats and some of the smaller lady drivers had to use wooden blocks on their pedals. One of the cars that I was allocated with was an older type Humber that had the habit of jumping out of gear at speed whenever I took my foot off the accelerator. I fixed this problem myself by attaching a piece of old inner tube, which acted like a strong elastic band, from the gear stick to the seat frame, which held it in place.

On another occasion when working in the pool, I was asked to drive Rab Butler, when he was Home Secretary and I was given his car to drive with the registration number, A120. This meant that when we drove around London all the police officers knew the number plate and who the car belonged to. But when the IRA became very active in London, the registration number was changed quite frequently, for obvious reasons. The Home Office was at that time in Whitehall, with the main door right opposite the Cenotaph.

One day when I was on duty driving the Home Secretary, all the newspapers were full of news about the police's most wanted man in Great Britain (I'm not sure what he was wanted for). I had just pulled up at the front door of the Home Office and the Home Secretary got out of the car and went inside saying to me, "I won't be very long and I need to go to the House of Commons". The police Sergeant on duty at the door asked me if I would like a cup of tea while I was waiting and I happily agreed.

We had our tea, and then as it was a nice sunny day, we stood on the front doorstep, overlooking Whitehall. Very soon afterwards, a man came up and said, "Would you mind if I have my photograph taken with you on the doorstep of the Home Office?" As he was a smartly dressed man and tourists were always asking if they could have photographs taken outside important buildings in Whitehall, the Sergeant said, "Okay". So he stood between us and we all smiled as a man who accompanied him took a photograph. He politely said, "Thank you." And off he went. We thought nothing more about it. Later that evening when the Evening Standard was delivered to the office, to our horror and great surprise, a large photograph of us was on the front page! It was of the most wanted man in Great Britain, posing between us. Obviously to him it was a great game to have managed to pose in front of the Home Office, although a bit embarrassing for us. But how were we to know as I certainly had never seen a photograph of him.

I also had the occasion to drive Harold Macmillan when he was Chancellor of the Exchequer. In 1956 I took him to the see ERNIE, the Premium Bond machine. We had a very interesting day and when we got back to London he handed me something and said, "I thought you might like this, so I've put it in your name." I looked down and saw that it was a premium Bond. I believe that it was one of the very first to be issued. I kept it for many years in my bedroom drawer, but unfortunately one day my house was burgled and it was taken with many other things. Luckily, they missed a sealed envelope containing

£1200 in cash. My son had obtained the cash for me to pay for a car I intended buying. He had written on the envelope, "This is a lot of dosh, Dad, mind you don't lose it." Obviously, the thief couldn't read, as he must have picked it up and thrown it on the floor, thinking it was just a letter!

The Government's Car Service was also responsible for providing the cars for the Commonwealth Prime Ministers' Conference. The Superintendent allocated me to drive the Prime Minister of Pakistan. I picked him up at London airport VIP suite. There were about five cars allocated to his party. I took him to Claridges Hotel where he was staying and I believe his party occupied the whole first floor. The next day I was confronted by one of our lady drivers, who complained that she should be the one to drive the President as she was senior to me. I agreed that she should drive him and I would drive his ADC, who was in charge of the whole party. He was called, Air Commodore Rabb. This was the best thing that could have happened to me as the Commodore and I got on like a house on fire. He was really down-to-earth. He told me that one of my duties would be to look after one of the President's family, who I believe was a princess. The Air Commodore introduced me to her and I was told to take her wherever she wanted to go (which was nearly always shopping). The first day that I took her out, we went to Harrods and other shops in Knightsbridge. In the afternoon when she'd finished shopping we went back to Claridges Hotel. When we pulled up outside the front door, she opened the glass partition in the car and thanked me. Then she emptied her handbag onto the front seat next to me said," That's for you", and to my great surprise I discovered there was at least £20 or more. That was two weeks wages to me! I opened the door of the car and she stepped out smiling saying, "Thank you. Come back the same time tomorrow."

To my delight, this routine went on for about three days. In addition, in the evenings I took the Air Commodore to different receptions. One day the Air Commodore Rabb came out of the hotel in a bit of a panic, jumped into the car and said, "The old Aga Khan has died. It's been announced that his grandson will be the new Aga Khan, rather than his son Ali Khan." It transpired that we now had to find his grandson, who I believe was a student in London, to tell him of the unexpected news. The Air Commodore had an address for him, which was in a block of flats near Notting Hill. After finding the block of flats, Air Commodore Rabb said he would like me to go up with him. So together we climbed up about two floors and knocked on the door of a flat, which was opened by a young man in a T-shirt and jeans. The Air Commodore announced himself and we were both invited inside. The young man asked if we would like a drink and poured us each a glass of orange juice. The A/C told him the news and said that he must put on his best suit as we had to take him to Buckingham Palace to be introduced to the Queen as the new Aga Khan. But the young man said, "But I don't have a very good suit." So I suggested that we take him to Austin Reed of Regent Street, the gentleman's tailors, to get him kitted out. They thought this was a good idea and off we went immediately.

He came out suitably attired and looking very smart. Then off we went to Buckingham Palace. When they came out, I was told that all had gone well. Soon after that the Commonwealth Prime Ministers' conference ended and I drove the Air Commodore to London airport. All the drivers lined up and the President came along the line and shook our hands. Each one of us was handed an envelope with £25 inside. Whenever I see the Aga Khan on the television or in newspapers, I wonder whether he remembers that very memorable day, when we knocked on his door and his whole life changed.

Another assignment that proved to be unforgettable was when I drove another United States general who I had to pick up from London airport (I was told he was in charge of Supreme Headquarters Allied Powers Europe, situated in Paris). I had to drive him with a police escort to Lloyd's headquarters in the City of London for lunch. The car I was given to drive was a Humber Pullman, with a glass partition which could seat three people in the front and four passengers in the rear. After lunch, I was parked outside Lloyd's main door waiting for them to appear.

As it was a nice sunny day, a very large crowd had gathered to see what was going on. The police motorcycle escort officer in charge, came up to me and said, "When the passengers get in the car and the doors are shut, I will drive off and I'd like you to leave immediately and follow me close up and fast."

I had two high ranking military officers sitting in the front next to me, as the car had a front bench seat, which obscured my view of the passenger door. However, I had two green lights on the dash of the car that lit up when the doors were opened and would go out when they were shut. So I had to rely on them and had to watch carefully for the lights to go out. The crowds in the street were all cheering loudly. With one eye on the police motorcyclist ahead, and the other on the little green lights, I was waiting intently to set off. "Bang" went the door shut and out went the green lights, so off we drove behind the police motorcyclist. The next thing, there was a lot of commotion and shouting, which I thought was from the crowds. But unfortunately the Lloyds doorman for some reason had opened the passenger the door again. (He must have thought it was not shut properly). He then found himself scooped off the pavement, and his top hat went flying as he clung to the door for about 50 yards. Luckily I'd seen that the green lights had come back on, so stopped the car immediately. He then shut the door once more, and off we went to London airport. When we arrived and my passengers got out, I thought I would be in the doghouse. But the General thanked the police and then came over to me and said, "Thank you very much for a memorable trip."

Two or three years later, I took a Cabinet minister to Lloyds for lunch and was taken to the restaurant where I joined some of the staff for lunch. After a while chatting with them they asked where I worked and I explained that I was with the Government Car Service. This seemed to spark their interest and they went on to tell me about one of their doormen's unusual experiences. They regaled me with the story of his close shave with one of our cars. Little did they know that they were telling it to the man who was driving the car at the time. And of course, I did not enlighten them!

The one thing about being in the drivers' pool was that you were never quite sure what your next assignment would be. One Friday afternoon I was in the garage polishing my car and heard my name on the tannoy asking me to go to the Superintendent's office. When I arrived there I was asked to take a seat. I was then asked if I would do a very important assignment and I was told that the President of Czechoslovakia was coming to the UK for a four week visit. The job would entail picking up the President at London Airport and taking him to various meetings with government ministers. The President had also said that he would like to go and visit Oxford, Cambridge and then onto Stratford on Avon as he was very interested in Shakespeare. There would also be another driver with a second car for his officials, which would be driven by a friend of mine called Billy Hall. I immediately agreed to this assignment and so the following week I duly arrived to pick up the President at London airport and took him straight to the Czechoslovakian Ambassador's residence in Hampstead, where I was briefed by one of the staff about the visit.

At the time of this visit, things were a little strained on the diplomatic front and the Czechoslovakian staff seemed to avoid talking to us and whenever I went to the Czech Embassy or residence it was always one particular man that discussed our movements for the day. The only other Czechoslovakian we met was a young man who drove the third car from the Czech embassy, but never spoke to us. At that time it was the custom whenever we went to a meeting at a Whitehall ministry, where we were nearly always waiting for two to three hours, that we would be asked if we would like cup of tea or snack. Usually I would agree to this and I would then go along to the Czech driver and ask him if he would like a cup of tea or a drink. Each time he declined, but to my surprise on about the fourth day of the official visit, the driver said, "Yes, please." So off we went inside the building and spent about ten minutes having our snack and drink before returning to our cars. I was surprised to find that the Czech driver spoke excellent English. We finished the day at an official dinner and then drove back to the Czech residence.

Billy and I had been asked to return again next morning at nine o'clock. We got there at about 8.30am when the Czech car pulled up behind us. I went to say good morning to the driver and was surprised to see a new face. I said good morning to him, but he did not answer. Later on that afternoon, I saw our government hospitality representative, who was in charge of the visit and said, "I see we've got a new Czech driver." He said, "Yes, the other driver has been sent home to Czechoslovakia for breaking the rules and talking to you." I felt really upset in case he'd got into trouble because of me as he seemed a really pleasant young man and we had only chatted about inconsequential things.

The rest of the trip went to plan and on the last night the embassy held a party for us in the basement of the embassy, to which all the police and foreign office staff, who had been involved in the trip were invited. Here for the first time many of the guests were introduced to Slivovitz (Brandy). It didn't take very long before the full effects of the drink were felt. Apparently the correct way to drink is was to have a large glass of what seemed to be soda water and then a small glass of Slivovitz. Perhaps some of the guests were forgetting the soda water because when Billy and I arrived at the party much later than everyone else, we were in time to see people being carried out and put into the back of vans and taken to sleep it off. Fortunately for us, Bill and I were driving so we just had a small beer and enjoyed the party.

The next day we went to the Czech residence to take the President back to London Airport return home. We were asked to go inside, where the President shook our hands and thanked us for a very good visit. Then he handed us each a box of 200 cigarettes. It was very good of him, but as I didn't smoke, I gave them away. The following week, the Car Service Superintendent told us that he had received a very nice letter thanking him for an excellent visit.

Of all the interesting people I drove, I should think the most famous one was Winston Churchill. Some years later, Margaret Thatcher was to say at the retirement party for her driver, Denis Oliver, who as a close friend had also invited me to join them, "My retiring driver Denis is probably the last surviving GCS man to have driven Sir Winston Churchill." But in fact, I had also driven him, if only from the House of Commons to No 10 Downing Street. I remember one evening that I was standing in the House of Commons courtyard waiting for my minister, when Churchill emerged. He looked around and asked me, "Have you seen my driver?" I said, "Yes, he is down at the canteen having his supper, sir". So, he said to me, "Alright, you can take me to Number 10". I said, "Certainly sir", opened the door, put him in and took him to Number 10. On his arrival, he said, "Thank you very much," and got out leaving me feeling very privileged to have driven such a famous man.

7 ALLOCATED TO DRIVE JOHN HARE (MINISTER OF LABOUR)

One day in 1960, the GCS Superintendent called me to his office and told me there was a vacancy for a full time allocation. He said it was to drive the Minister of Labour, John Hare. His office was at 7. St James Square. The first question I asked was, "What has happened to his regular driver?" He told me that the minister had sacked her. But I found out afterwards that she had asked to come off the job, as he was a very difficult man to work for, which I was soon to find out for myself. Driving John Hare was to be the worst experience of my 46 years of service in the GCS. However, I agreed to give it a go as it was the first step on the ladder to my ambition, which was to hopefully one day to drive the Foreign Secretary. This was always classed as the best job in the GCS because, amongst other things, one of the great perks was that you would accompany the Foreign Secretary as his baggage master when he travelled the world.

My allocated job with John Hare was to pick him up near Regents Park, where he lived and take him to his office in St. James Square, Westminster. There were two routes to get there. Either you could go down through the squares, or through the parks. But if I had decided to go down through the parks he would say, "Why are we going this way? I wanted to go through the squares." So if I preferred to go through the squares, I would say, "Through the parks sir?", and he would automatically say, "No, through the squares." And this was how I managed to go the way I wanted to go.

Usually, I had to pick him up at his Regent Park home and he nearly always asked me to be there at 8 am. Sometimes he would keep me waiting for an hour or more before coming out. The butler would sometimes call me over to the basement side window and give me a cup of tea, but I would have to keep close to the wall as he said he would be in big trouble if Mr Hare was to see me having a drink.

One day, I thought my luck had changed, because he said he was going to the Epsom Derby and would I like to go with him. He said he would be driving his Bentley and I could keep an eye on the car at the races. He then told me to meet him next day, outside his garage which was quite close to his house near Regent's Park. I arrived there nice and early with my sandwiches and a drink. After a while, he came out of his garage in his car and stopped next to me and just said that he had changed his mind and would not be taking me. He told me to pick him up next day at the usual time at 8 am and simply drove off, leaving me standing at the side of the road.

He had another little trick he used to play with me. On Mondays, if he came in by train from his country home, I would have to pick him up at Liverpool Street station. He would usually come out with his bags, accompanied by a porter carrying a large bucket of water full of flowers. He would then place the bucket on a large sheepskin rug on the floor of the car, which was an Austin Princess limousine. I then had to drive the car from Liverpool Street station to Regents Park, which is quite a long way through heavy traffic. But this had to be done without the bucket falling over, which was practically impossible. We both knew that the bucket was going to fall over. Nevertheless, it gave him a good reason to shout at me and call me a useless driver.

However, it wasn't just me who received the harsh treatment. One day his male secretary came out of the office in St. James' Square to go to the House of Commons. The messenger was holding the rear door of the car open and the secretary got in first. We waited for a few moments for the Minister to come out. Unfortunately, whilst the secretary was sitting on the rear seat, he unwittingly rested his hand on the door jamb. When the minister got in, the messenger quickly shut the door, crushing the secretary's hand in the door jamb. He let out a loud scream, and the messenger quickly opened the door. The secretary was in a terrible state, as there was blood everywhere. But the minister just said, "Get out, you're making a mess." As soon as the poor man had got out of the car, John Hare told the messenger to shut the car door. Without further ado, he ordered me to drive on to the House of Commons as he was going to be late.

At least I had some good news towards the end of that year, 1960, when I returned home for dinner one day and my wife told me that she was pregnant with our first child. Much to our delight, the following year in July my first son, Kevin, was born safely at home as planned and my mother and father were ecstatic to have their first grandchild.

A few weeks later I took two weeks leave from work as the minister was going on his holidays and we decided to go off for a trip to Ireland as my wife's mother came from there originally. So off we drove with our new baby to Fishguard in our brand new car, a Ford Consul, which was a real pleasure to drive and caught the ferry. We decided to do the Ring of Kerry route and also call in to see my wife's relatives, which turned out to be very interesting.

The first relative we dropped in to see was an uncle who regaled us with stories about the times they called 'The Troubles', between the I.R.A and the British Army. As we sat listening, he told us about the time he had been approached by the IRA, who had given him a rifle and told him that he had to shoot his brother because he was in the British Army. He had no alternative but to agree to their request at the time. However, immediately, he left Ireland and came to England where he joined the British Army and served in it for 20 years.

Later, we all went off to the local pub or bar. As we pulled up, I looked around and saw that it was a large area about the size of two football pitches with very large trees about every 50 yards around the perimeter. I remarked that it was a beautiful area. The uncle looked at me and shook his head saying, "This is where a terrible massacre took place." I looked shocked and said, "When was that?" He replied," Oliver Cromwell was responsible for it." I was surprised that such an ancient atrocity was treated as though it had only recently happened. I said, "Oliver Cromwell didn't just do this to the Irish but also to many an Englishman. In fact, I believe he even hung his own brother for disobeying an order!" I think my words fell on deaf ears. Nevertheless, we had a really good time together and met some very nice people and altogether had a most enjoyable holiday.

At the time I was driving John Hare, he was being harassed by a very large lady called Mrs Benson, who held him responsible for the fact that she was not getting a pension that she thought she was entitled to. (This is what I was told, anyway). She would wait for him outside his office front door and shout at him and wave her umbrella. She seemed to be there nearly every day. After a while it was decided that as there was a back door, I should take the minister that way in. However, it didn't take long for the lady to tumble to this and sometimes she would be standing at the back door. So, I used to approach the office slowly from St James's Square and check which door she was at before deciding where to stop. It was a bit of a cat and mouse game as she was a very crafty and determined lady. One day she managed to get into his office on the second floor and tried to attack him. Luckily, his messenger managed to get in between them, but not before getting hit in the face with a telephone! I could never understand why Mr Hare didn't get the police involved.

The side entrance to the Ministry of Labour also had a large garage or loading bay with a steel roller door and I was told to put the car in the garage if we were going to be in the office for more than an hour or so. The side door messenger would pull up the shutter when I arrived and I would park my car by backing it into the garage and go through the side door to the office. One day I was told that Mr Hare wanted to go to the House of Commons straight away. So I had to go and get the car and bring it round to the front door. Off I went, down to the unlit garage and got into the car. The messenger pulled up the roller shutter, and I drove out of the garage to go round to the front door of the Ministry. As I had to turn left, I looked in the rear view mirror to see if it was all clear. To my horror and disbelief I saw Mrs Benson sitting in the rear seat, who I hadn't noticed in the garage because it had been so very dark and also there was a glass partition between the front and rear section. I pulled up at the front door and called the doorman over. It took both of us to pull her out of the car. I just could not understand how she managed to get into the Ministry and find her way to the garage.

It all came to a head when I had to take the Minister to his country home on the Friday evening. It was very late in the evening and dark when we arrived. John Hare got out of the car, and I followed with the official red boxes. He was just about to open the door when we heard crunching footsteps on the gravel behind us. To my amazement when I turned round I saw it was the woman from hell again; Mrs Benson! She rushed up to us and thrust her umbrella at the Minister. However, it missed him but pierced my jacket, narrowly missing my stomach before sticking into the door. I then realised that it had a sharp point and could have caused a very serious injury. She pulled out the umbrella, turned round and without a word disappeared into the night. So after this I decided enough was enough and on the Monday morning I went to see the Superintendent of the GCS. I told him what had happened and said I would like to come off the allocation. He just looked at me and said that he was amazed I had lasted as long as I did, in fact from 1960 to 1962.

8 DRIVING LORD DRUMALBYN (MINISTER OF PENSIONS) & FIRST INTRODUCTION TO MARGARET THATCHER

I was relieved to be off the job and was very soon reallocated to Lord Drumalbyn, Minister of Pensions, whose office was in John Adams Street, off the Strand. He was another ex-high-ranking army officer, but a very quiet and easy-going gentleman who I got on with very well. He quite liked to walk to the House of Lords and wasn't very demanding.

While I was at the Ministry of Pensions, Lord Drumalbyn's PPS was Margaret Thatcher. She had her own little private car, (I think it was an MG), which she kept in the downstairs parking area of the Ministry, which was just off the Strand. One day I was waiting for the Minister at the front door to take him to a meeting when Mrs Thatcher came out and asked me if I would take her to the House of Commons. I explained that I could not, as the Minister could come out at any minute before adding, "Why don't you use your own car that's downstairs in the garage" and she replied, "The battery isn't very good. I think it's flat again".

So I quickly made the decision to ask the doorman if he would keep a lookout for my Minister and if he came out, just say I had to go to the men's room. I grabbed another messenger and we all went downstairs to her car. She jumped in and we gave it a push start. Luckily, the car started straight away and off she went to the House of Commons. I ran back upstairs, just as the Minister, Lord Drumalbyn came out. .

To save me any further hassle, the following day I went out and bought a new battery which I fitted to Margaret Thatcher's car. When she came out later that day, I went up to her and said, "I've fitted a new battery to your car". She was absolutely delighted, thanked me and paid for it. It was soon afterwards that there was a government reshuffle and she was made Minister for Education and allocated her own official car.

Another of my exciting assignments was when President Kennedy came over to England in June 1963 and I was asked to drive the fourth car in the cavalcade, as Lord Drumalbyn didn't require me that weekend. We went to many places in London without incident, but when the President was due to leave England from Gatwick airport, we stopped off at Prime Minister, Harold Macmillan's home, near Forest Row. As there were about twenty cars in the cavalcade, it was impossible to get into the driveway of the house, so most of us had to park in the lane outside. Because of the importance of the occasion, nearly all of us were driving new Austin Princess limousines. But, unfortunately, we did not know that nearby there was a large group of CND demonstrators who had found out where we were. No sooner had we parked up when we heard the sound of people shouting and around the corner at the end of the lane appeared what looked like hundreds of angry people carrying their 'Ban the Bomb' placards. We numbered about 20 drivers and 10 police officers.

We thought the demonstrators would just shout and show their banners. However, they decided they wanted to destroy our cars and cover them with CND slogans in white paint. Luckily we were in a narrow lane and reinforcements arrived soon afterwards. But by then our cars were in a very sorry state. I remember that the car next to mine was driven by Tom Wade, who I believe had served in the war as a commando. After he had dealt with the first two or three who attacked us by throwing them through the hedge, they gave him a wide berth.

Fortunately, as the lane was very narrow, the police were soon able to get control of the road and the demonstrators, who were held back at the bottom of the lane and things gradually settled down a bit. We picked up our passengers and set off to the airport. President Kennedy personally thanked all of the drivers and gave us each a tie-pin, which was a model of the torpedo boat he commanded during the Second World War. I still have this memento today as a reminder of a very interesting experience.

Whilst driving Lord Drumalbyn, there was a very sad occasion when his young daughter, who was out walking (I think it was on a coastal path) disappeared and was never found. The shock of this tragedy contrasted with my own good news of the birth of my second son, Neil, in 1963. Again my wife had decided to have a home birth, but this time things did not quite go to plan. Soon after the midwife had left us after her regular visit, my wife went into labour late at night. I telephoned the midwife from a neighbour's house but before she could get to us, I had started to deliver the baby myself! Fortunately, she arrived as I was attempting to unravel the cord from the baby's neck, but I felt reassured when she said I had done a very good job, although I think my wife should take most of the credit! Two years later when my third son, Andrew, was born at home, it came as a relief that everything went to plan and with no problems.

In the government reshuffle in 1963, I lost the allocation to drive Lord Drumalbyn and was allocated instead to drive Niall MacDermot, Financial Secretary at the Treasury. His previous claim to fame was the fact that he was the QC who prosecuted the Great Train Robbers. (It just goes to show what a small world it is, that I was allocated to drive the QC who prosecuted the 'Great Train Robbers' and once lived next door to the girlfriend of one of them, Buster Edwards).

Niall MacDermot was a very tall and handsome man with film star looks. But he was also a very kind gentleman. For example, when my dog died he told me to go and buy a new dog and he would pay for it. I got on with him extremely well from the start. We both shared a passion for art and he was a great collector. He went to several galleries and I was flattered that he asked my opinion when he looked at the pictures he was considering. Unfortunately, he was more interested in modern art, whereas I was more interested in classical art. I think I upset him slightly on one occasion when he paid out quite a lot of money for a picture that to me looked like a lot of scribbles on a canvas. I think it was called the "Queen upon her Throne" I told him that it looked as though it had been drawn by a monkey. He looked a bit upset and called me a Philistine, but smiled and didn't hold it against me. In fact, when he bought himself a new top of the range Rover car for his personal use, on the occasions he went on holidays, he would give me the keys and say, "There you are Peter, you can use it for a couple of weeks".

Life was not always so carefree at this time. For example there were two unhappy events which took place when I was working with Niall MacDermot. The first was when a large block of flats collapsed in the East End of London killing a number of people. I drove him down there as he had been asked by the Prime Minister to assess the very sad situation. Even more daunting was our trip to Aberavon in Wales when the slag heap collapsed killing many people, including children who had been in their school. On both these occasions I had to drive Niall to the sites of the disasters to see what help could be given and it was heart-breaking to see the devastation.

On a lighter note, one day whilst I was waiting for him at the entrance to the Treasury, I started chatting to the security guard. During our conversation, a lady walked in and showed her pass before continuing inside. To my amazement, it was no other than Mrs Benson, who had caused the Minister of Labour and me so many problems in the past! I spluttered, "But that's Mrs Benson", to which the guard replied, "Yes, she works here in the canteen". At last I knew how she had been able to gain access to the Ministry of Labour, her pass allowed her access to any Ministry.

One weekend Niall MacDermot turned up unexpectedly at my house in Streatham with his fiancée and introduced me to her. She was a Russian interpreter and seemed very pleasant. He had been quite impressed that I had my own house, as I was the only driver in the GCS at that time who had actually bought their own home. Instead, everybody's ambition was to live in a council flat. In fact, I was told by other drivers that I was mad for putting a millstone round my neck. The house had cost me £2000 and I had great difficulty in getting a mortgage and raising the £350 deposit. My mortgage was £12 a month and my wages were approximately £12 a week. How prices have changed!

Soon afterwards, Niall MacDermot, married his Russian interpreter fiancée, and I wondered whether this might have cost him his job, as he lost his position in the Government reshuffle at about that time.

I was then reallocated to Fred Willey at a newly formed ministry called the Ministry for Land and Natural Resources. This Ministry was in a building in Whitehall, called Guydear House. On the first day I picked up Mr. Willey from his Hampstead home and took him to his new Department in Whitehall. We parked outside the front door and walked up the steps into the front hall. Mr Willey then realised that the only staff in his Ministry was his secretary, myself and the messenger who opened the door! Gradually, day by day, more staff turned up until he had a fully working Ministry, although it never became a very big Department. I understood that his main job was to revise the leasehold laws. He was a very quiet man, not the sort with whom you could have a friendly chat. The Labour government at the time did not have a very big majority. I think it was about three. There were quite a few all-night sittings. I have known Fred Willey to come out of the House at seven in the morning when the house rose and then I would drive him to his Hampstead home. This was after I had sat in the car in the House of Commons car park all-night. We would pull up outside his home where he would go in to shower and have his breakfast. He would then come out again and say, "Back to Whitehall." He didn't even offer me a cup of tea!

At about this time, if there was a vote in the House of Commons, MPs had to be in the chamber to vote within eight minutes of the Division bell sounding. As well as the bell ringing in the various Ministries, the nearby pubs and restaurants also had a division bell fitted. If a division was expected, which could come at any time, the driver would sit outside wherever the Minister was eating and if the Division bell went off, his Minister would rush out and jump into the car. The car would then race to the House of Commons. The police were also waiting and when they saw our cars coming flat out with headlights flashing and horns blowing, they would hold up the traffic for us to get through. Eventually the decision was taken to change the system before somebody got killed! However, at that time MPs' attendance at the House was so important, because the government had a small majority, that they even transported people by ambulance from hospitals and parked in the House of Commons courtyard as their vote would be counted as long as they were on the premises. This was a very stressful time, but there were no accidents getting to the House to my knowledge!

One evening while driving Fred Willie back to his Hampstead home he told me that one day the following week he wanted me to drive him to King's Cross railway station to catch a train to Sunderland, which was his constituency. Apparently the local government were building, I believe, a new Town Hall and he explained that he had been asked to lay the foundation stone for it. Since the rules for Ministers at that time were that they could only use the official car up to 50 miles from Whitehall, unless they were in a job which had police protection, he said he would catch the nine o'clock train from King's Cross station.

I knew that Mr. Willey was not a very good timekeeper. So I said I'd pick him up at about 7.45 a.m. from his home, which I knew would give us sufficient time to get to the station. The day arrived, and I got to his home at about 7.40 a.m. and rang the doorbell. The door was opened, and I was told that Mr. Willey was just about to have his breakfast. So I went back to my car and read the newspaper. However, when it got to 8.15, I started to get a bit agitated, as it is now the rush hour. So once again, I went back to his house and rang the doorbell. I said, "If we don't go now sir, we will miss the train." Five minutes later, he came out and said he was unhappy with me for harassing him.

Fighting back my feelings of irritation, we set off on a journey and got as far as Hampstead High Street, before coming to a halt as the traffic was not moving. It soon became very obvious that we would miss the train as it was now 8.50 and we were not even halfway to the station.

I could hardly believe my ears when Fred Willey said to me that we should have left much earlier! I pulled over into a side road and said, "Do you want to go to your office now sir?" He replied, "No, I want to go to Sunderland." He continued to explain that the foundation stone had been inscribed with his name and today's date on it and also all the officials, including a military band, would be waiting to greet him. I explained that I was not allowed to go more than 50 miles from London, without authorisation from my Superintendent. However, I said I would be willing to take him if he took responsibility and said that he had ordered me to take him. He just said "Yes, yes, let's go."

So off we went and once I got onto the A1 main road, there was no motorway at that time just dual carriageway, I put my foot down and drove flat-out. I had to stop just once for petrol and Mr Willey bought me a bottle of orange. Fortunately, the new building we were heading for was on the main road just before we got to Sunderland.

As we arrived, we could see people forming up for the ceremony. Mr Willey apologised for being a bit late and eventually the stone was laid, while I managed to get some food at the reception. We then had to set off back to London, but this time we had a more relaxed ride.

The next day, the Superintendent asked me to go to his office and inquired why I had broken the rules and driven to Sunderland without permission. Fortunately, after I had explained the situation, he said he would write to Mr. Willey and I heard no more about it.

After a very busy year, I was looking forward to a break from work. It was Christmas Eve and I was about to leave the House of Commons after being told that I would not be needed until after the Christmas recess. Just as I was getting into my car, I was approached by a police officer who was on duty in Speaker's Courtyard who said, "Are you finished?" I replied, "Yes, I am going to put my car away at the GCS depot, then I'm off home." He said, "Could you do me a favour and drop off a Minister who lives nearby. His driver has gone home and the Minister has had a little too much to drink." I said, "Okay as long as he goes now. I want to get home."

The police constable disappeared into the House of Commons and within a couple of minutes came out with a Labour Minister, who I recognised but had never driven, and another police constable who was helping him to walk. I opened the rear door of my car and after a bit of a struggle managed to get the Minister inside. I was given his address and fortunately it was only about half a mile away, just off Victoria Street.

However, when I arrived at the address I couldn't park as there was no space to pull into and had to drive about a hundred yards past the address before I could find anywhere to park. I opened the car door and then realised I had a big problem. My passenger had not only drunk too much, but was now out cold. He was a big man who must have weighed about 17 stone.

After a difficult struggle I managed to get him out of the car and onto my back. Giving him a fireman's lift, I carried him to the front door of the address, which was a block of flats. I rang the bell and the door was opened by a porter, who said, "Oh not again" and beckoned me inside. I carried the Minister into the hallway asking, "Where do you want him?" The porter pointed to the corner of the hall and said, "Over there will do." So I just let him drop down in a heap. The porter said, "Thanks. Have a good Christmas" and I turned and made my way home.

One morning a short while after Christmas, I had just arrived in the office when I was asked to take Fred Willey straight to No.10 Downing Street. There was news that the Torrey Canyon oil tanker had foundered in the English Channel and Fred Willey was given the job by the Prime Minister of overseeing the cleanup operation. I was told we would leave almost immediately and be away for quite a while. As I did not have time to go home, I went along to the Army and Navy Stores in Victoria Street and bought the essentials that I thought I would need for at least a week away. We set off immediately, with the Minister and his secretary heading to Portsmouth, where we were told to go straight to the Naval Headquarters in order to get the latest information on the situation.

When we arrived at our destination, the Naval Headquarters, we were met by a large number of high-ranking naval officers, who were expecting us. We got out of the car, and one of the officers said to us, "This way gentleman, please." As no introductions were made, the officers were not quite sure who was who. We were then taken inside Naval Headquarters, where we were told that dinner was about to be served.

We were taken into a very imposing room, where we were to be seated at a very large table, which was covered with silverware. A voice announced, "Please be seated gentleman." There must have been at least twenty very high-ranking naval and army officers. I was amazed to see that behind every seat stood a naval rating, so that when you sat down, he immediately held a menu in front of your face and asked what you wanted. On each side of me was seated a high-ranking officer and I now realised that I was in the wrong place, but thought, "What the hell, I'd better just go along with it." I was asked by the officer on my left what my position was in the Ministry. So I said I was part of the Minister's staff and just left it at that. By smiling and nodding at the correct places in conversation and keeping my answers short, I was able to get through the meal successfully.

When eventually the dinner was finished and we all got up and were told to go into the next room for drinks, I was very relieved. I looked around and saw the Petty Officer in charge and asked if I could have a word. He took me into another side room where I told him that I was the Minister's driver and asked if he could find me somewhere else to eat as we were going to be there for two days. He looked at me in absolute amazement and said he had been in charge of the Officers' Mess for quite a number of years and he'd never known anybody under the rank of naval captain to sit at that table! He then invited me to join him in the Petty Officers' Mess, where they had quite a laugh at my predicament, but seemed very impressed that I'd managed to carry it off.

Two days later, the Minister decided that he wanted to go further along the south coast to see what environmental damage had been caused by the oil spillage. We drove on along the coast, stopping here and there, until we reached Swansea, where the Minister's secretary back in London had already booked us into the Red Dragon Hotel. It was about six o'clock when we parked up and went to the reception area inside and got the keys for our rooms. The Minister said that we should meet in the dining room, at eight o'clock for dinner. So I went up to my room and discovered to my surprise that it was very luxurious. I washed and freshened up and then went down to the dining room, where we were joined by, I believe, the Mayor and a couple of other dignitaries. We all sat down at the dining room table, and Fred Willey asked me if I had a decent room, to which I replied that it was absolutely beautiful as it had a piano, a writing desk and fruit and flowers. He looked at me and said, "Well, that's a lot better than mine!" The penny dropped. He'd got my room and I'd got his. We had a good laugh, but he did not ask to exchange rooms as we were only there for two nights and the move would have been too much hassle. I couldn't believe my good fortune.

9 LIFE IN THE FAST LANE WITH RICHARD CROSSMAN (SECRETARY OF STATE FOR HEALTH)

Soon afterwards there was a government reshuffle and the Superintendent called me into his office to say that Richard Crossman had been made Secretary of State for Health. However, he wanted to change his driver (who was a lady driver who did not want to do long hours or long distances travelling) and said he would prefer to have a male driver instead. Would I be interested? I was a little apprehensive as Richard Crossman had a bit of a reputation for being rather quick-tempered and did not tolerate fools easily, but I said I would give it a go anyway. The next day I went for an interview at his office. He put me at ease straight away and made it clear that he wanted most of all loyalty and dedication to the job. He asked if I could start the next day, which I did. He was very proud to tell me of the fact that he was now in charge of the biggest department in the government with the largest budget. I soon found to my delight that I got on extremely well with him and also his PPS, Tam Dalyell, and discovered that as I got to know him better he liked to tell me about his previous experiences before the war.

He spoke fluent German and during the 1930s he had spent some time living in Germany and I believe had actually married a German lady. But he soon discovered, when the Nazi party came to power, that he completely disagreed with their politics. As his wife was a staunch Nazi supporter, he divorced her and came back to live in England. When war was declared, he told me that he used to broadcast propaganda to Germany with the actor Marius Goring. He played the part of a German officer and Goring played the role of the Sergeant. It was the equivalent of Lord Haw Haw's propaganda broadcasts to Britain. Although he never told me, I think he must have been an intelligence officer during the war because he told me that if the British captured a German spy, he would sometimes interrogate them. This took place in a building which is next door to the Savoy Hotel in London. I asked him whether the British ever tortured these captured spies. He said no, it wasn't necessary. If we couldn't get anything out of them we would tell them that if they weren't going to talk, we would hand them over to the French for interrogation. "Usually, they gave the information needed straight away," he said with a smile, "I wonder why?"

After Germany's surrender, Crossman told me that he was sent there to interrogate high ranking German officers. While he was over in Germany, he was told that the British had found a list of names of people to be shot if the Germans had occupied Britain and his name and Marius Goring were quite near to the top.

There were many memorable events during the time he was Secretary of State for Health. For example, there was one occasion when he decided he needed to see the Prime Minister, Harold Wilson, urgently. So I drove him to 10 Downing Street to see him, where I dropped him off at the front door. As I was turning the car around, I noticed to my surprise that Crossman had come straight back out. He jumped into the car next to me and very angrily said, "Let's go back to the Ministry. I haven't been able to get past that Secretary, Marcia Williams and his driver. It seems as if they're running the place." I think he was right about this, as Harold Wilson's driver went everywhere with him. I remember one time having a cup of tea in the House of Common's restaurant with his driver, Bill Housden, who was bragging about the time he joined the Prime Minister in the helicopter that flew out to H.M.S. Fearless at the time when Rhodesia was negotiating its independence.

We also went to Chequers on occasions for cabinet meetings, which were usually held on a Sunday. There was one particular time in 1966 that we had to go there as King Hussein of Jordan, who was on a state visit, had been invited for lunch. He was expected to arrive at twelve o'clock midday, so all the drivers and protection officers were waiting by the main door of the house to get a closer look at the honoured guest. However, when it got close to one o'clock and there was still no sign of the King, everyone became a bit anxious and was hoping that nothing had happened to him on the way. Finally, to everyone's relief, we saw in the distance his car cavalcade coming up the drive. The King's car drove up to the front door and he got out. He made his apologies for being late and went into Chequers.

The Prime Minister's protection officer went up to the King's car and said to the driver, "Glad you're here; we were getting a bit concerned." The King's driver said that on the way to Chequers, they had stopped at a set of traffic lights when an E-type Jaguar pulled up alongside them. The King had put down his window and spoken to the driver of the E-type. He then got out and asked the driver if he wanted to sell his car. After a while, the owner of the Jaguar agreed. I think he was made an offer he could not refuse!

I also remember another occasion when Jim Callaghan was Prime Minister and he was holding a cabinet meeting at Chequers. It was a very nice sunny day, so all the drivers decided to have a game of cricket on the green just outside the house. One of the drivers who was playing was called Albert Willis, who was a real full of life character. He was an ex-army man, and I believe he had served in the North African desert. He had shown us photographs of himself when he was part of a team of men who went behind enemy lines blowing up ammunition dumps and causing havoc. But his only problem was that he found it difficult to say a few words without using Anglo Saxon expletives!

On this particular day, when we were having a game of cricket, Albert was getting very excited, and his colourful language was flowing quite freely. Suddenly a window of the house opened and Callaghan, shouted, "Albert, could you keep the noise down we're trying to hold a cabinet meeting here!" Albert apologised saying he would try his best and after this short interruption we carried on with the game. Only a character like Albert, who was well known for his dedication to the job and well liked by all the ministers he drove, could get away with it.

On another occasion, after a cabinet meeting, we left Downing Street and we had another passenger with us in the car, I believe it was Anthony Jay, who was to become one of the writers of the famous television programme "Yes Minister." As we were driving along Whitehall, I said to Richard Crossman, "Have you heard of any of the appointments in the government reshuffle?" He said, "No". So I said to him. "I know of one at least, Barbara Castle has been made Minister of Labour" Crossman said, "No way. I don't believe it. Where did you hear this?" And I said, "From a very reliable source, her driver." When I heard a similar line used in "Yes Minister" some years later, I like to think it had some connection to that conversation that had taken place in our car.

It was while I was driving Richard Crossman, that I was called to do jury service at the Old Bailey, which was quite an interesting experience. I sat on two cases; the first trial was about a man, who had robbed passengers on a double-decker bus. This case was quite straightforward, with lots of witnesses and he was found guilty. I was then selected to go on to another case, which was a bit more complicated. It concerned an armed robbery at a supermarket in Fulham. There had been two armed robbers with shotguns, which were fired into the ceiling in order to get staff to hand over their cash. However, there had been a tip-off to the police who were expecting them. As they were caught red-handed, they had pleaded guilty. The man we had to try was the getaway driver, who had been waiting just around the corner. He pleaded not guilty and said that he thought his friends were just going into the supermarket to buy cigarettes and a few groceries. The prosecution asked him about the shotguns, but as both guns had been sawn down and fitted into a small holdall, he said he hadn't known they were there. However, when the police searched the car he had been in, they found a set of different number plates. The police then discovered the number plates were from the same make of car he was in and had been reported stolen a few days earlier.

The trial lasted for about two days while all the evidence was presented and finally we were sent into the jury room to decide the verdict. That was when we realised that some of the jurors were deciding whether the defendant was guilty or not guilty by his appearance rather than by the evidence. When the defendant was first brought into the court and stood in the dock, we had seen a very smartly dressed and quite good-looking young man with a big smile. The first vote was nine 'guilty' and three 'not guilty', with all three 'not guilty' votes from lady jurors. After a few more hours spent going over the evidence again and again, the vote was 11 to 1. The one lady, who still voted 'not guilty", kept saying that that the defendant looked too nice to do anything like taking part in an armed robbery. After another long session of examining the evidence regarding the car, she changed her mind and the defendant was eventually found guilty.

The two men who had used the shotguns were given five years imprisonment and the driver was given four years. When the men's previous records were read out in court, it turned out that the driver was a really vicious thug with a long criminal record. When I spoke to the lady juror who had held out to the end, she looked at me and said, "It just goes to show you can't go by looks!"

In the course of his job as Secretary of State for Health, Richard Crossman was very keen to visit as many hospitals and health centres as possible. On one occasion, I took him to a new clinic in the east end of London. It was opened in order that drug addicts could go there and get an injection for hard drugs. I think the idea was that every time they went, the dose was lowered and they hoped to wean them gradually off the habit. Altogether there were three official cars plus our car. We parked alongside a type of pre-fabricated building. The patients would go in one door and after their 'fix' would come out of the other end of the building. It was a very nice day and all the drivers were waiting near the exit end for their passengers. The door opened and three or four men came out. I remember one man, who still had his used hypodermic syringe in his hand. He looked at us and then turned to his mates and said, "No wonder the country is in a state with this lot 'swanning' around in their flash cars."

We covered many miles doing these types of visits and often went on long-distance trips. On one occasion, after I'd only been driving him for a short while, Crossman said to me. "Will you pick me up at six o'clock tomorrow morning?" I explained to him that it would be very difficult for me to get there by six o'clock as Government Car Service drivers were not allowed to take their cars home. He looked at me for a few seconds before picking up the telephone and calling the Superintendent of the Car Service and telling him that he would like me to keep the car at home seven days a week with immediate effect so he could call me out at any time. When Crossman asked for something he tended to get it! I then had to explain to him that it would be very difficult for him to get in touch with me because I didn't have a telephone as I could not afford to have one installed. Once more he said, "Okay" and picked up the 'phone again and rang the GCS and told them that it was very important for me to be contactable at short notice. He told them to have a telephone fitted immediately at my home. The word soon got around amongst the other Cabinet Ministers drivers and soon afterwards all Cabinet Ministers drivers had phones laid on at their homes. In addition, most of them were able to take their cars home if they were on standby.

Richard Crossman's country home was at Cropredey Bridge near Banbury. When he went home at weekends, he nearly always took the train if possible, from Paddington. But if we were going on to visit a hospital, I would drive him home, and he would put me up at his house so we could drive on next day for his official appointments. He had a lovely family, including an attractive wife and a very intelligent young son called Patrick and a daughter called Virginia. They always treated me like one of the family and invited me to join them for meals.

One Friday evening when we arrived, I discovered that he had about six American friends staying with him as guests for the weekend. After dinner he stood up he said, "Tomorrow morning, everyone's going for a swim in my outdoor swimming pool". He looked at me and said, "Including you, Peter." I was a bit taken aback as it was wintertime and quite frosty outside. However, I didn't take it too seriously until the next morning when the door of my bedroom opened and Crossman threw in a pair of swimming trunks and said, "Downstairs, in five minutes." As I didn't want to let the side down, I put on my trunks and went downstairs. But it turned out that only the two of us were standing there, Crossman and me. We trotted across the frozen grass, pulled back the cover of the supposedly heated pool and dived in. The water was only lukewarm, and we probably did about four lengths of the pool. Richard Crossman got out and I followed. However, the worst bit was to follow as we had to go back over the frozen grass. I glanced up at the top-floor windows of the house to see the smiling faces of his American guests peering out. They must have thought we were completely mad, although I'm sure this episode made a good impression on them and no doubt succeeded in conveying Crossman's strength of character. At least I played my part and didn't let the side down.

The next day we set out for an official appointment, which I think was near Leeds. So we left Banbury nice and early in order for us to be at our destination for lunch. Unfortunately, there had been a major accident on the main road, and we were diverted quite a long way round. I realised that I had to drive flat out to get him there in time for lunch. We eventually arrived about ten minutes late. As we pulled up and got out of the car there were dignitaries gathered waiting to greet him, including a very high ranking police officer. Richard Crossman said he was very sorry to be late because of an accident on the main road and that his driver, pointing to me, had been driving at 100 miles an hour to get there on time. At this, the police officer looked at me and said, "That's a very serious offence." But I said, "No, it just felt like 100 miles an hour, but I made sure I kept to the limit!" Luckily, he just shrugged his shoulders and left it at that.

Crossman even included the incident, in his book, "Richard Crossman. Diaries of a Cabinet minister, volume 3", when he said,

"I had Peter Smithson, down here last night. He is a marvellous fellow absolutely devoted. He buys everything for me, goes everywhere, he will mend our house for us, he is the biggest handyman in the world, as well as being the biggest butler-footman. He is everything to me. This morning, he drove me up to Leeds in an hour and 50 minutes averaging 100 m.p.h. on the motorway"

After the official greetings, we walked up into the main reception hall, where there were about 200 people already seated at long tables for their lunch. As he was walking up to his place on the top table, Richard Crossman turned to the organiser and said, "Where are my secretary and driver sitting?" The official said that he was sorry but he hadn't realised that he was supposed to cater for us. So Crossman said in a very loud voice to the whole seated assembly, "Everybody, move your chairs closer together so we can get two more seats in on the end." Immediately everybody stood up and shuffled their seats. It was quite embarrassing to watch everybody picking up their cutlery and plates and rearranging them on the table. We got a few looks of annoyance, but nobody ever argued with Richard Crossman!

It was at about this time that the Labour government, which was in power but had a very small majority, had many late-night sittings in the House of Commons. Sometimes if Richard Crossman had been in the House of Commons all day, he would come out with his PPS Tam Dalyell and say that as he'd been in the House all day he needed to walk home to get a bit of exercise. He would ask me to take his official red box home for him and, as I had a key, I would do this for him. He lived in Vincent Square, which was about 15 minutes away.

One night the house went up at about 12.30 a.m. and Tam Dyell had already gone home to Scotland. By the time Crossman came out of the House of Commons it was about 12.45 a.m. He got into the car in Speakers Courtyard and straightaway I could see that he wasn't very well. I asked him how he felt and he said he didn't feel too good. I drove him to his home and when we arrived I got out of the car, took his red boxes out of the boot, ran up the steps to his front door and opened it with my key. Crossman seemed to have difficulty getting up the steps and into the hallway. I was putting his red boxes on the desk when I heard a loud thud. I ran to the hallway and found he had collapsed and seemed to be unconscious.

Richard Crossman was a big man and must have weighed about 18 stone, but I knew I had to get him upstairs to his bed. After a lot of effort, I did manage to get him onto his bed and undressed him. I covered him up but he seemed to be shivering and also had a very high temperature. I looked around the house and found two hot water bottles, which I filled and put into his bed. I then looked into his bathroom cabinet but all I could find were some aspirins. I managed to get him to take two but by now I knew he needed a doctor as soon as possible. However, I decided I should really ring his wife up in Warwickshire first to let her know the situation. I got through to her and she said she would ring his doctor straight away and get him to call an ambulance. In addition, she asked if I would stay with him until she arrived and I immediately agreed.

Soon afterwards an ambulance appeared and he was taken to Westminster Hospital and put into intensive care. I stayed in his home until Anne Crossman arrived in the early hours of the morning. She told me the next day that the doctor had explained to her that if we hadn't got her husband into hospital that night, he could have easily died since he had a type of pneumonia.

I spent a lot of time going between his office and the hospital and it wasn't long before he became his old self again. As soon as he came out of intensive care and had started on the road to recovery, he began to run his department from his hospital bed. Then, after being released from hospital, he went home to Warwickshire, where he continued to run his department, as he gained his strength. As soon as he was fully recovered, he returned to his office at the Ministry of Health. One day as I was driving him to his London office, he said to me, "Would you do me a big favour?" I just said, "Yes, if I can. But what is it?" He said, "I have three American friends to whom I would like to give dinner at Vincent Square, but privately. I would like you to prepare the meal and serve it for me." I said, "But I've got no experience of doing that kind of thing at all." He said, "Don't worry, what you can do is go to Fortnum and Mason's in Piccadilly and get the meals. They'll be all prepared and all you've got to do is heat them up. I can give you a list of what to get." I said, "Alright, I'll give it a go, but I can't guarantee it will be a success."

The next job I had to do was to find the cutlery and crockery equipment. I found that the cupboards in the kitchen were full of things that I don't think had been used for years. This meant that I had to clean everything before they could be used because, to my knowledge, Richard Crossman never had a meal in his London home in Vincent Square. He nearly always ate at the Carlton club or the House of Commons.

About a week later, the big day came and off I went to Fortnum and Mason's and picked up the food. I remember the menu was a special soup starter they had made, followed by a main meal of chicken and vegetables, finished with a selection of cheese and biscuits. I had already found some very nice bottles of wine in the kitchen. I set the table very carefully, and Crossman seemed quite impressed with the look of it. His guests arrived on time, and I gave them an aperitif while I prepared the food for the table. After a while I told my boss that the meal was ready and he took everybody into the dining room. Once the meal was finished and the guests had left, Crossman thanked me and said it had been a very successful dinner party.

During the time I was driving Richard Crossman, he told me that he was in the process of writing his 'Crossman Diaries'. However, he added that they would not be published while he was alive. I was delighted to find that when they were eventually published he had given me thirty five mentions.

One of the quotes from his "Richard Crossman. Diaries of a Cabinet minister, Volume 3", that I will always treasure is an entry for 7 May 1970,

"I was going to have a haircut at nine o'clock, but I waited at Vincent Square until 9.10, when one of the girls telephoned to say that Peter Smithson had been held up by some accident that had caused a two-mile queue. It made me realise how utterly I rely on him. He must be the most intrepid, skilful and vigorous driver in London. He is absolutely reliable, always turning up on time, and I'm going to miss him when I cease to be a Minister."

Crossman had two children, Patrick and Victoria. During the school holidays he would quite often bring Patrick, who was about eleven years old at the time, with him to London and I was pleased to take him to a museum and show him around the London sites in my free time. Patrick was a very intelligent young man and very well mannered. I became very fond of him and looked forward to his company. One day, Richard Crossman told me that he was going to bring Patrick with him the following week and wanted to take him to the cinema to see 'The Battle of Britain', which he was keen to see. As it was on a Saturday, he suggested that I should also bring two of my three sons, so we could all go together to see it and then have a meal afterwards on him. This we did and we enjoyed a very memorable evening together.

Crossman recounts this event in his diaries in an entry for 31st December 1969,

"Anne brought the children up in time for lunch and then Peter Smithson very kindly asked them to tea with his children at his house in south London. This evening, he brought them back with his two eldest boys and off we all went up the Tottenham Court Road to the Dominion Theatre to see the film 'Battle of Britain'."

It was at about this time that my parents moved to West Byfleet, where my mother was the canteen manageress to a firm of architects and my father also got the job as their handyman and caretaker. They were given a bungalow to live in on the site. The company they were working for had moved into a big Victorian mansion, which had the River Way running past the garden area and a large Victorian boathouse that was empty. I decided that it would be very nice to have a boat. However, as I could not afford to buy one, I decided that I would build one.

At the time I lived in a small house in Streatham, South London, where I knew I would have to build it. Unfortunately it only had a small back garden, but there was a narrow back lane just big enough to get a car down. So first of all, I built a kind of garage that was a bit flimsy, but kept the area dry. I designed the boat with a speedboat hull, but added a cabin at the rear. I built it this way for the safety of the children on board. I fitted it with a 20 hp outboard engine and called it the PETROKAN, which was a mixture of my name and the children's initials. It took me about a year to build the boat, which had a hull made of marine ply and then covered with glass fibre. When it was in the water, it looked like a small cabin cruiser, although appearances were deceiving. I remember that soon after it was built, I took it down the River Way and into the river Thames. It was a lovely day and we were just gently cruising along, when a large catamaran came up behind us and the man steering it blew his horn while sitting sipping a drink. He gestured to us to get out of his way, but I just opened up the throttle and we took off. My boat skimmed across the water, leaving the man who had blown his horn looking flabbergasted as we skipped over the water at high speed. We had many good trips up the river at weekends and I kept the PETROKAN for about three years. I sold it when my mother and father left Byfleet and consequently I lost my mooring.

A few years later, after Richard Crossman had died, I was driving Reg Prentice when one day I heard the sad news on the radio that his son, Patrick, had committed suicide. So at the first opportunity, I went to see Anne Crossman at her country home. She told me that she could not understand why Patrick had done it. He had just passed all his examinations, so she had bought him a car for his birthday and for doing so well. She told me that she had gone out shopping and couldn't get back into the house on her return as it was locked. Eventually she managed to get in and found Patrick had hung himself from a hook in the kitchen ceiling. She thought it was perhaps because he missed his father so badly and hadn't got over his death. I was very upset because it was a tremendous waste. He was such an intelligent, pleasant lad, who I believed would have made a big success of his life.

10 HIGHS AND LOWS WITH RICHARD WOOD (MINISTER FOR OVERSEAS DEVELOPMENT)

In 1970 there was a General Election, which was won by the Conservatives and I was reallocated to Richard Wood, who was made Minister for Overseas Development. I was absolutely delighted with this allocation as Richard had a reputation as being a very nice man to work for. He was always immaculately turned out and whenever he went to the House of Commons he would dress the part and wear a black jacket and pinstripe trousers. In addition, whenever he was going to make a statement in the House, he would ask me to get him a carnation for his buttonhole. He was a very easy man to get on with and always treated his staff with kindness and consideration. He had lost both his legs at the age of 22 when he was with the Army in North Africa. However, this did not hold him back from having a full life with his devoted wife Diana.

When he was Minister for Overseas Development, his office was on the ninth floor overlooking St James's Park. I had a room a few doors from his office and on occasions he would call me down to discuss his movements for the week. I remember one occasion when I went in to see him and he was sitting at his desk with his back to the window overlooking the St. James' Park. As we were talking I noticed in the distance a large cloud of black smoke. I pointed it out to him, and we started looking for landmarks to try and pinpoint what looked like an explosion. We came to the conclusion that it looked as though it was near the city (it turned out to be the Old Bailey). After a short time, we noticed another explosion and this time it was much closer. This turned out to be at old Scotland Yard at the top of Whitehall.

One day when I was standing in Speakers Courtyard at the House of Commons, I got chatting to the police officer in charge of the area about the explosions I had witnessed with my boss. We eventually got onto the subject of Airey Neave and the terrible tragedy of how he had been blown up by the IRA. The policemen told me that the IRA had planted a bomb on the underside of Mr. Neave's car whilst it was parked outside his flat in the Victoria area. The bomb had been fitted with a mercury switch that would go off if the car would go down or up a slope. They must have known that he used to park his car in the House of Commons underground car park, so as he drove down the ramp in his car, the bomb exploded and Airey Neave was killed.

The police officer went on to say that it was only by luck, and due to a mistake by the IRA, that's another disaster with a bomb didn't take place. He went on to explain that one day, as he was leaving new Scotland Yard in Victoria, he noticed an old car parked just outside the main door. (In those days you could park anywhere you liked as long as there was no yellow line on the road). One thing that caught his eye was that the car, although very old, had a very modern number plate fitted. He decided to have a closer look at the car and saw that it was crammed full inside with something on the rear seats, which was covered over with a large blanket. He called the bomb squad, who found it was full of explosives. If they had gone off, it could have been a disaster, as the New Scotland Yard building is all glass and the explosion would probably have sucked out the glass and anyone inside with it.

These were very hard times for Richard Wood, as it was during the period when there was a 'three day week' due to the many workers' strikes taking place. Because the electricity supply could be shut off at any time without warning, we were told not to use the lifts. This was a bit difficult for the Minister as it meant climbing up 18 flights of stairs on his two false legs, so he found it quite a challenge. However he managed it and I never heard him moan.

It was also quite challenging times in the House of Commons, as I believe the Tories only had a majority of about three then and needed all their MPs to vote. I remember that Richard had to go to a conference in Belgium. So for the next three nights, I used to visit London airport at about nine o'clock to collect the Minister. As soon as his plane landed, I would meet him at the aircraft where he could get into my car and we would drive straight to the House of Commons and into Speakers Courtyard. However, he never got out of the car. As soon as the division bell went at 10 o'clock, we drove straight back to London airport where he caught his flight back to Belgium. This went on for three nights. I asked the Minister why he never got out of the car. He said that it was not necessary because anyone considered ill or in some way disabled could apply to the Chief Whip for this concession and as long as you gave your word that you had been driven onto the premises and away again, you would be counted in the vote.

On another occasion, Richard had to go to Brussels for a meeting. As he also had to visit various places en route, including Luxembourg and Paris and because he was disabled, he was allowed to take his official car and myself as his driver.

After arriving at our hotel in Brussels and checking in, an official car arrived which we were told to follow to the building where he was to have his meeting. I remember that it was a very complicated route. On arrival, he got out of the car and I parked up, fully expecting to have to wait for some time. However a few minutes later, Richard reappeared and said "Peter, I've left some papers back at the hotel. I wonder if you would go and fetch them for me." So off I went retracing my route back to the hotel and found the papers. Unfortunately, when I began my journey back to the building where the meeting was taking place, I found it quite difficult to find the route again, as previously I had simply followed the official car and Brussels is quite a busy and complicated place to negotiate whilst driving a car. In addition, I did not know the name of the building or the street where I had left him, fully expecting to be able to simply follow the official escort car there and back. However, I did remember that there was a statue of Winston Churchill outside the building. As I didn't speak any French, I found it even more difficult to ask for directions to a place whose name I didn't know. Fortunately one of the people I stopped to ask spoke good English and recognised the name 'Churchill's statue' and with various arm gestures, pointed me in the right direction. Much to my relief, I eventually found the correct building and was able to reunite Richard with his papers.

As we were spending a lot of time in the Ministry at Victoria during the time of the three-day week, I used to pass quite a bit of my time in the messengers room, which was just a few doors away from the Minister's office. Unfortunately, it was quite small, so I decided to have a chat with the office keeper to ask if he had any other spare rooms on the ninth floor. I explained that I needed to be quite close to the Minister in case he needed to leave the building quickly, as I would always have to carry his red box. He said that there was a room opposite the Minister's office that was used as the teleprinter room, so we went and had a look inside. After moving one or two pieces of equipment around, I finished up with a table, a chair and about 6' x 8' of space next to the window. This would do me fine, I thought. I remember that the lady messengers here were all very kind and whenever they made the Minister a cup of tea or coffee they also brought me one as well.

It was soon afterwards that the Minister's secretary said to me, "Why don't you join the Civil Servants Art Club as you have the perfect place to paint here?" I thought this was quite a good idea. So that weekend I visited my father and told him what I intended doing. He said to me, "That's a coincidence. It's your birthday soon and I've already bought you a present, you might as well take it when you go home." He then put a box on the table and told me to open it. To my surprise, it contained a full set of oil paints and brushes and everything you needed to paint an oil painting. I was absolutely delighted and took the painting kit with me to work on the Monday. When I showed it to the messenger ladies, one of them said to me, "You ought to join the Civil Service Art Club straight away because they hold an exhibition and competition every year in the main conference room and there are some very nice prizes."

So off I went to the art shop, which was just around the corner and bought a couple of canvases. I started to do a painting but it was not very successful as I'd never painted in oils before. However, about a week later, one of the messenger girls came into my room and said, "I thought you might like this." It was a lid from a chocolate box with a picture of a farmhouse with lots of apple trees in blossom. By this time, I had in fact joined the Civil Service Art Club and promised them that I would be showing a painting at their next exhibition, if I could get it finished in time. However, since it was only a few weeks away, I had to work full on, and by basing my painting on the picture I had been given, managed to get it finished just in time to meet the deadline.

The big day came around and the exhibition room was quite crowded as the judge entered the room. He talked a little about art and his likes and dislikes before starting his tour around the room, looking at the entries and making a few comments here and there. When he got to my painting he said a few kind words and then continued along all the other paintings until he arrived at the last entry. He then made a short speech saying he was quite impressed with the artwork and that he had picked a winner. To my great surprise he went back to my picture and stuck a label on it, which just said, 'Winner.' He then turned to the people in the room and said, "Who painted this?" I was still in shock and just said, "Me." He then asked how long I had been painting, to which I answered, "Not very long," as I didn't have the nerve to say four weeks! Anyway, I had certainly caught the bug for painting and took my painting materials with me to work for the next 25 years.

While the 'three-day working week' was on, the unions were trying to get as many members to go on strike as possible. As the drivers in the Government Car Service were mostly members of the Transport and

General Workers Union, I reluctantly became a member, although I was certainly not a great supporter. This came to a head one day, when the union called a meeting to say that union headquarters had been in touch and wanted all the drivers to support the strike and refuse to drive the Government ministers. This was to be the first occasion that I had stood up and spoken out at a union meeting. I said, "I won't join the strike, because if we go on strike and the Ministers are not driven by the GCS, the police will immediately take over. Once they get in, it will become a permanent arrangement and a lot of us will be out of a job."

The union had a vote and the result was not to support the strike action. Soon afterwards, the GCS, offered some of the drivers the opportunity to take early retirement or redundancy with large cash package deals. I think most of the union representatives accepted the deal and left the Government Car Service. So much for union solidarity!

Another interesting thing happened when I was driving Richard Wood. One evening, Richard said that he wanted to go into the House of Commons to pick up some papers and that he would only be a short time. I said I would go and have a quick cup of tea. As I went back into Speakers Courtyard, a car was driven in and parked across the front of my car. The driver jumped out and went into the House before I had a chance to say we were just about to leave. A few minutes later, Richard came out and said, "Okay, let's go." I replied that a car was blocking us in, as I hadn't had time to tell the driver that we were about to leave. Richard asked if I knew the man's name. I said, "No, but I can tell you who he looks like. He looks just like Tarzan with long flowing hair like Johnny Wuissenmuller." Richard had a good laugh and went back into the House of Commons, where apparently he told some of his friends what I had said. He soon came back out again, saying he had found the driver and he was going to move his car. "His name is Mr Michael Heseltine. It was the hair that did it and made him quite easy to find!" The name 'Tarzan' was to become famously attached to Michael Heseltine from then on.

It was at about this time that Richard and his wife Diana decided to buy a villa in the south of France, near Ste Maxime. Soon after they had got it furnished, they very kindly offered it to me and my family to use on two or three occasions.

During the time I was driving Richard Wood, one of the main things I had to do was to make sure I always had a spare pair of his artificial legs in the boot of the car. I remember one amusing incident when he arrived from his Yorkshire home by train. He would always make his way down the corridors to the front of the train until he was close to the engine, so that when the train came to a standstill, I would be opposite his carriage door. On this particular occasion, the train stopped and he stepped out of the carriage, but unfortunately there was a small patch of oil on the platform and as soon as his foot went on it, his leg slid from underneath him and snapped his artificial leg at the knee. He landed on the platform, with one leg over his shoulder. I knew I had a spare pair of his artificial legs in the car, so I grabbed a porter's trolley and helped Richard onto it and then proceeded to take him to our car. As I wheeled him towards the station entrance where the car was parked, we got some very funny looks from passengers when they saw this immaculately dressed man sitting on the porter's trolley with one leg over his shoulder and with a big smile on his face!

One day, when I was driving Richard Wood I said, "I hope you don't mind me asking, but how did you lose your legs?" I trust I've now got the facts right, as it was a long time ago that he told me. He explained to me that he was serving in the army in Libya, North Africa, during the Second World War and was in the desert when they were attacked by German Stuker dive Bombers. After the attack, Richard and his men were starting to collect together any undamaged equipment when the Stukers returned. Thinking that lightning didn't strike the same place twice, he took refuge in a bomb crater. Unfortunately, another bomb did hit the same crater and landed on Richard's legs, luckily not exploding, but taking off both his legs below the knees. I understand that his Sergeant carried him quite a long way to get him to a first-aid post and this must have saved his life. However, because of the long journey back, the doctors then had to take both his legs off at the knee.

Richard had been quite a tall man at 6ft 4ins. He said that the hospital fitted him with a pair of artificial legs as soon as it was feasible. Unfortunately, once they were fitted and he stood up they realised that the new legs were not long enough, as his hands were nearly touching the floor! He told me, good-humouredly, that everyone had had a good laugh as he explained that he looked like an ape. But that was just typical of Richard. For the whole time I was his driver, I never saw him in a bad temper, or to be miserable.

The Woods showed their unbelievable kindness to me in many ways. For example, one day when I arrived at their home, Diana had just got back from the Peter Jones store in Sloane Square and was feeling very pleased having bought a tin of white emulsion paint, which she explained, they were selling at half price. It has to be remembered that in the 1970s, emulsion paint was quite expensive. I said I thought that was a bargain and I would go there after work and get a tin for myself. Soon afterwards Diana went out but quickly returned and said, "Here you are Peter, it's a gift from me," and handed me a 5 litre tin of emulsion. I couldn't believe that she'd been all the way back to Peter Jones to buy another tin of paint just for me!

In addition, if we were out and about, with Richard going from one meeting to another, Diana would say, "We need something to eat." So we would pull up at a restaurant and she would say, "Lock the car up Peter, you're coming in with us for a meal."

I was very proud to be Richard's driver and it was a very sad day when the Conservatives lost the general election that year and we parted. However, Richard did go on to the House of Lords, taking the title of Lord Holderness.

It was an even sadder day when I heard of his death and attended his funeral at the Guards Chapel at Wellington barracks off St James's Park. However, his widow, Diana, still keeps in touch with me and has been very kind in advising me with my memoirs. She even invited Angela and me to her home recently for lunch and a helpful chat as she is a Private Publisher of Wilton Press, which she was for many years with her husband, who started the business more than 23 years ago.

11 TROUBLED TIMES WITH REG PRENTICE (MINISTER OF EDUCATION)

At the next election, the Labour Party was returned, and I was allocated to Reg Prentice, the new Minister for Education, whose office was at Waterloo next to the station. My time with him was very dramatic to say the least. I found out that he liked his football and supported Crystal Palace. On a few occasions he kindly took my son, Andrew, with him to watch them play. Reg was a very easy man to get along with and even asked me to call him Reg in private and only use his formal title when in official company. But unfortunately, he had a lot of problems with the left wingers in his constituency, who tried every trick in the book to get rid of him as their MP. When he attempted to get some support from the Prime Minister, Harold Wilson, he was simply told that he must try harder to please them.

He used to go to his constituency nearly every Saturday, which was in Newham, East London. He had a lot of support from the older constituents but the hardliners were bringing in a lot of left-wingers from all over the country and getting them into the community so they would have a majority to vote him out. I remember they would bring in busloads of militants and put them into houses so they could vote against him. They decided to put up a man called Kelly, from Leeds, to stand against him as MP. This man had left his wife and children and owed quite a large sum of maintenance but they thought he would be a better MP than Reg Prentice, who was one of the most dedicated members of Parliament I had known! I remember one week, he said that the next Saturday he was going to have a big meeting in a hall so that he could speak to as many of his constituents as possible. He asked if I would help out by being a steward, hand out leaflets and show people to their seats. I knew he needed all the help he could, so readily agreed, not know what I was letting myself in for!

On the day of the meeting, we got to the hall nice and early. It started to fill up quite quickly, mostly with the older generation who were all very supportive of him. About a half an hour before the meeting was due to start and the hall was nearly full, the rear doors burst open and what seemed to be dozens of men all shouting and screaming abuse, flooded the back of the hall. The chairman of the meeting asked them to calm down and then they could have their say but in an orderly fashion. This just made things worse as the mob started throwing bags of flour and what seemed to be old apples. The first few rows were full of older people who got the worst of it. The bags just burst opened when they hit anybody and they were finding it very hard to breathe. The meeting ended very quickly as people got out as fast as they could. I managed to get to Reg, who was also covered in flour and got him out through the rear door. Fortunately, I had anticipated trouble and parked our car a street away. When we reached it, I was pleased to see that the mob hadn't found it. So I put him in the car and drove him to his home near Croydon.

On Monday it was back to the office as usual. He said to me that he did not think he could go on much longer. I already knew this as I could see that events were taking their toll on him, both physically and mentally. He was no wimp, as he had served in the Army as an officer and had a very strong character. Soon afterwards, I took him to a meeting with the Prime Minister, Harold Wilson, but he didn't seem to get much support and came out a bit dejected as he had been told by the Prime Minister that he was 'under par'. That evening at the House of Commons he asked me to come to his room. When I got there, he was with his friend Brian Walden. Reg handed me an envelope addressed to the Prime Minister and said, "Will you take this to No.10. It's my resignation. Then come straight back here."

I delivered the envelope to No. 10 and returned to his room. As I went in, he said, "Open the drinks cabinet. Let's all have a drink while we wait for the Prime Minister to call." I poured out a couple of stiff whiskies for them and had a small beer myself as I was still on duty and would be driving. About ten minutes later, as expected, the phone rang and it was the Prime Minister. Reg spoke to him for about five minutes and then put the phone down. He said, "He's asked me not to resign, as it could cause a run on the pound. He also said he would give me more support in the future."

However, as things continued to get worse, Mr Prentice offered his resignation twice more. Very soon afterwards his resignation was accepted and also from the Labour Party as well. He crossed the floor and joined the Conservative party. This also affected me because I was temporally without a Minister. However, not for very long as I was soon invited to drive the Minister of State at the Foreign Office, Lord Goronwy Roberts.

12 LIVING THE HIGH LIFE

LORD GORONWY ROBERTS (MINISTER OF STATE AT THE FOREIGN OFFICE)

The GCS Superintendent asked me to go and see Goronwy Roberts for an interview at his office in the Foreign Office. I thought this was a bit odd as, normally, you just turned up and took over from the previous driver. However, it turned out that the Minister was not happy with his present driver as he didn't like working long hours. I knew that the Minister of State at the Foreign Office was a very demanding job, as there always seemed to be a reception every night at one embassy or another. Lord Roberts' official responsibility was the Eastern bloc, including all the Communist countries. I found Lord Roberts to be a very nice man to work for and very congenial. One day, soon after I started, he said to me, "As you are usually so very well turned out and smart, when I go to official reception, I would like you to come in with me." He explained that by doing so, I would be able to get something to eat and also keep an eye on him, so that when he was ready to leave he could give me a signal and I would go up to him and say, "Don't forget Sir, you have to be at your next meeting soon." He could then say his farewells, and we could leave.

I also noticed that no matter which Communist country's embassy we went to, there would always be the same waitresses and staff. Whenever we went into the embassies, Lord Roberts always used to introduce me as his aide. One of Lord Robert's favourites was the East German Embassy. I remember one evening we went to this Embassy and as we went through the main entrance, Goronwy said to me, "I'm going to the gents, see you inside the reception". So I walked up the main staircase and was met at the top by the German Ambassador, who said, "So nice to see you. Do come in Mr Smithson". He continued, "Is Lord Roberts with you?", and I replied, "Yes, he's just washing his hands." I was amazed that he had remembered my name and had even thought that I would be there without Goronwy. He would have been even more surprised if he had known I was his driver!

I enjoyed driving Goronwy very much as he was more like a good friend that my boss. He even invited me and my family for a weekend at his Welsh home and took us to see Portmeirion.

About a week later when we were back in London, he came out of the Foreign Office and told me that evening we would be going to pick up a lady from her hotel and taking her for dinner. So later on, we drove up to the Dorchester Hotel and he went inside to collect her. For diplomatic reasons, I won't say who she was but she was a very important high-ranking foreign lady. When she came out with him, I saw that she was absolutely stunning. She had beautiful red hair and a fantastic figure and she was wearing a beautiful tight-fitting blue evening dress that was covered in sequins, and around her neck was draped a long white boa. She could be a match for any film star. He put her into our car and asked me to drive to Victoria.

When we arrived at our destination, he asked me to pull up outside the 'Spaghetti House'. They got out of the car and as he helped the lady out he said to me, "Lock the car Peter and come in with us." To my absolute shock and horror, we proceeded to walk inside the 'Spaghetti House'. It was the kind of restaurant where you took a tray and walked along the counter and took your food. So we helped ourselves to our food and you could have heard a pin drop in the restaurant as all the other customers stopped eating and just stared at us in disbelief. The meal was over very quickly and she asked to go back to The Dorchester Hotel. When we arrived there, she just got out of the car and went inside without a backward glance. That was the last time I saw her.

At that time in the Government Car Service many of the lady drivers had been there for many years and seniority meant an awful lot to them. Woe betides you if you were given a job that they thought they were entitled to. On one occasion, when I was driving Goronwy Roberts, there was a Polish conference held at Lancaster House that Goronwy Roberts was chairing. The conference lasted nearly a week and at the end of it, the Polish Ambassador decided to have a reception at the Polish embassy to thank everyone involved. There were about five or six lady drivers allocated to drive the Polish delegates. On the last day of the conference, the GCS lady driver who seemed to be in charge, came up to me and said with a bit of a smirk, "I don't know if you've heard, Peter, but all of the allocated drivers have been invited to a reception at the Polish embassy. But as you were not driving a delegate, I'm afraid you have not been invited." I just said, "Well I hope you have a good time."

On the day of the reception, Goronwy said to me that he would be going to the reception and that he wanted to go fairly early. When we arrived we were about the first there. Goronwy turned to me and said as usual, "Park the car and come in with me." We both walked through the front door and were met by the ambassador and his staff. He greeted us and said, "Come in gentleman, and have something to eat and drink. While Goronwy was chatting to the Ambassador, I moved across to the table where the food was laid out and picked up a plate and took some of food and was then handed a nice glass of wine by the waitress. I looked round the beautiful big hall and saw that there was a lovely garden at the back. I walked across to the window, which had long net curtains, and pulled back one curtain to look outside and saw several ladies turning around to look at me. I realised that they were the GCS drivers having their sandwiches outside under a canopy. I held up my glass to greet them with a smile. The look on their faces when they saw me was unbelievable and I will always remember the occasion with much satisfaction.

On another occasion, it was Australia Day and we had to be at the church in the Strand, St Clement Danes, which is opposite Australia House. When we arrived, we were a bit late and the church was completely full, but they had kept two seats in in the front pew for Goronwy and me. We walked down the aisle, through the full church and took our seats in the front row. Goronwy was sitting on my right hand side, next to the aisle. Directly in front of us, standing at the lectern not more than ten feet away, the Archbishop was preaching, looking directly down on us. The sermon went on for quite a long time and it was very warm in the church. This was all taking its toll on Goronwy who was gradually starting to close his eyes and lean towards the aisle. It got to the point where I actually thought he was going to fall into the aisle. The priest, who was giving the sermon, couldn't take his eyes off him. Every time Goronwy was about to fall, he paused the sermon and I would grab him and pull him back upright. This went on for about twenty minutes when, to my relief, the sermon ended. We were then asked to sing a hymn. As the music started Goronwy suddenly leapt to his feet, held up his hymn sheet and started to sing as if he had been listening to every word.

There was a General Election in 1979. So while it was taking place, I took a holiday in France but made sure I kept my eye on the news to see how the election was going. As soon as I saw that the Conservatives had won, I knew that I would no longer be driving Goronwy-Roberts and rang the GCS to speak to the Superintendent. I realised that as I was number three in seniority in the car service that meant that I should be allocated to drive the Chancellor of the Exchequer. However, I wanted to make sure that the job would be mine as it would be a few days more before I returned home. I knew that if another driver got in first, they might try to hang on to the job. Luckily, the Superintendent had anticipated this and put a lady driver on the job who did not want an allocation, as it could easily be a full-time, seven-day week occupation. The following Monday, after my return home from holiday, as I picked up my car from the GCS garage, the Superintendent handed me an envelope which contained a reference from Goronwy-Roberts, which was extremely flattering.

From: The Rt. Hon. Lord Goronwy-Roberts.

House of Lords · Westminster

25 June 79

Mr Peter Smithson.

Mr Peter Smithson was my ministerial driver from December 1976 until May 1979, when I ceased to be Minister of State at the Foreign and Commonwealth Office on the change of government.

Throughout this period his efficiency and dedication were outstanding. He not only displayed the skill of a first-class driver. He also studied my programme every day and week with immense care in conjunction with my private office and other officials, all of whom consistently paid high tribute to his intelligence and alertness.

My movements were often complicated and under pressure – for instance, the constant commuting between the Office and the House of Lords and other offices in Whitehall, visits to official gatherings at Embassies (sometimes three or even four in one evening) and journeys to airports, often when there was very little time to spare. Mr Smithson was instantly at hand, and had always anticipated every contingency. He literally never failed me at any hour of the day or night, and as a result he made my work as a very busy Minister much easier than if I had had to concern myself with details which normally I would expect to check.

As a result I very soon came to regard him as an aide, as well as driver, and invited him to accompany me to receptions, where his wide reading and and thoughtful conversation were real assets. His deportment and discretion were always beyond praise.

I regarded him as I do now as a friend and colleague. He is blessed with a charming and able wife, and his family are among the most attractive that my wife and I have ever met.

I shall be very glad indeed to stand as reference for him in any connection.

Goronwy - Roberts.

Deputy Leader of the Opposition; Opposition Spokesman on Foreign and Commonwealth Affairs; late Minister of State, 1964-70, and 1974-1979.

G-R/3.

My father, security guard, outside the Treasury

At the Czech Embassy with Billy Hall

My self-built boat PETROKAN on River Way

At No 11 with Angela Rippon, Anna Ford, Denis Davey & Ester Ranzen

Budget Day with Denis Davey (Doorman at No 11), Lady Howe & Sir Geoffrey Howe

With Sir Geoffrey Howe, Lady Howe and staff outside No 11, Budget Day

Sir Geoffrey Howe in robes of the Master of the Mint, with John (later Lord) Kerr, 1982

Presentation of my BEM by Sir Geoffrey Howe at the Foreign Office, 1984

Sir Geoffrey & Lady Howe leaving No 11 before presenting the Budget

My Jaguar XK120 when it arrived from the U.S.A

Jaguar XK120 after I had finished the restoration

Completely restored XK120, 140 & 150 & some of my grandchildren

13 ALLOCATED TO SIR GEOFFREY HOWE (CHANCELLOR OF THE EXCHEQUER)

I immediately drove off to Kennington to introduce myself to Sir Geoffrey Howe, who lived in a house in Kennington, South London. I rang the front doorbell and it was answered by Sir Geoffrey himself. I said, "Good morning, sir. I'm your new allocated driver." Little did I know then that I would be driving him for the next 24 years. But once again, I was extremely lucky and met one of the nicest gentlemen I have had the privilege to work for. In the course of time, I was privileged to meet his delightful wife, Lady Howe, and their family and also his housekeeper, Mrs King, who Sir Geoffrey was later to refer to in his memoirs as," … our treasured housekeeper at four different houses."

We left his home soon afterwards and went to the Treasury in Whitehall, where he introduced me to his private office staff. A couple of weeks later we moved into No. 11 Downing Street, where I met the Doorman, Dennis Davey, who was also Sir Geoffrey's personal messenger and we became very good friends as we spent many hours together. Dennis really knew his job and was the ideal person for it.

During my time at No. 11, from May 1979 to June 1983, there was hardly ever a dull moment as many famous people passed through the door and I had the privilege and pleasure of meeting them. For example, on one occasion Princess Margaret had been invited to an evening dinner party. There was quite a gathering of people in the hall, including myself, who wanted to see her close up. Her car drew up outside No.11 and Dennis went out and opened the car door and showed her into the hallway. He took her fur stole and she walked through with a smile, looking extremely elegant, before being greeted by Sir Geoffrey and Lady Howe. That was the nearest I had ever been so far to royalty.

On another occasion, one Christmas, Dennis opened the door and there, to my surprise, stood three of the most famous presenters on television at that time: Angela Rippon, Anna Ford and Esther Rantzen. They had come to help out at one of the many charity events organised by Sir Geoffrey and Lady Howe, who both gave a lot of their time to support various charities. At this party, Sir Geoffrey would dress up as Father Christmas and come down the staircase and hand out presents to a gathering of disabled children, who had been enjoying the company of the gathered celebrities. After a while, I became quite used to the visits of important and famous people at No. 11, who were quite often popping in to see Sir Geoffrey or Lady Howe.

Whenever Sir Geoffrey was working on his budgets I had quite a lot of spare time. I had managed to get a small room for myself on the ground floor where I used to do my oil-painting. It was normally used as a security room and my car was parked conveniently just outside the door in the courtyard. Whenever Sir Geoffrey came down to go to the House or wherever, his office didn't bother to ring me to tell me he was on his way down as he liked to just open the door and say, "Alright Rembrandt. Let's go" and he'd have a look to see what I was painting at the same time. Sometimes he'd have one of his visitors or friends or even a Minister with him, and I'd feel quite honoured to have such distinguished people taking an interest in my art work.

One of Sir Geoffrey and Lady Howe's best friends was the famous actor Sir Donald Sinden and on occasions he and his wife would stay for the weekend at the Howe's Warwickshire home. Quite often, we would go to see a play at the Shakespeare Memorial Theatre in Stratford-upon-Avon and Sir Geoffrey would sometimes ask if I would like to go in with them. I always enjoyed this treat and I remember that it caused quite a stir and turned a number of heads to see Sir Donald sitting in the audience with Sir Geoffrey.

One of the best things that happened to me when I started to drive Sir Geoffrey was that he and Lady Howe, who were great dog lovers, had just got a Jack Russell puppy, who was named 'Budget' by the family, for obvious reasons. He became quite a celebrity, appearing in many newspapers and before the Chancellor's Budget Day speech in the House of Commons, was photographed and televised being taken for a walk in the park by Sir Geoffrey and Lady Howe. He was a very good natured little dog and spent a lot of time with me so we became very great pals.

Sir Geoffrey came from the Welsh town of Port Talbot, which also produced Richard Burton, Anthony Hopkins, Catherine Zeta Jones and the ex-Speaker of the House of Commons, George Thomas, later to become Lord Tonypandy. On one occasion, I took Sir Geoffrey down to Port Talbot to receive the 'Freedom of the City'. We stayed with a relative, Kathleen Pollard, whose father had been a very famous sea captain, during the Second World War and had brought a very badly damaged oil tanker, which had been attacked by the Germans, safely into port. He was honoured and decorated and a film was made of the incident.

It was soon after starting to drive Sir Geoffrey that one day Dennis and I were sitting inside No. 11 having a cup of tea when there was a knock on the door. Dennis went to open it and, standing outside, there was a young man with blond spiky hair and wearing a rather grubby white suit. He said, "My name is Alec and I'm Sir Geoffrey's son." We were a bit apprehensive but Dennis invited him inside. Alec explained that he had difficulty getting up Downing Street to No. 11 because the police didn't believe that he was who he said he was.

I said to him, "Where on earth did you get that suit. You look like somebody from the film Casablanca?" He replied quite proudly, "It cost me two shillings and sixpence off a market stall." We were also later to learn that his hobby was playing the drums. It just goes to show how first impressions can be misleading, as I was to find out that he was an extremely well educated and a very likeable young man, who was later to become a very successful businessman and I'm proud to say that I am still very good friends with him and his family to this day.

His twin sister, Amanda, and her husband, Steve, were also highly educated and successful in their respective careers and in addition extremely pleasant and friendly towards me. Ever since their wedding, to which I was invited, they have remained good friends and I was always invited to join them whenever the Howes visited their home for dinner, where they always made me most welcome.

One memorable incident that Sir Geoffrey himself mentions in his autobiography happened on his journey to Brussels for his final December 1981 meeting when he was President of ECOFIN (EC Council of Finance Ministers). I drove him and John Kerr, the Principal Private Secretary, to Gatwick airport VIP lounge. We arrived nice and early for the flight. Sir Geoffrey asked if the flight would be taking off on time, but was told by the lady in charge of the VIP suite, that the Governor of the Bank of England had not yet arrived. A short while later, as the Governor had still not arrived, Sir Geoffrey was told by the airport official that they had given his plane a later slot.

Eventually, the Governor arrived and said that he had been driven to the wrong VIP suite. So, they were quickly hurried onto airport-side cars, which would take them to the aircraft. As they left to drive off to the plane, we noticed that it had started to snow quite heavily. So much so that we were eventually told that it was not possible for the flight to take off. However, by this time most of the other drivers, including the Governor of the Bank of England's driver, had left. By then the weather was so bad that the Gatwick train service had also been suspended as well. I had stayed at the VIP's suite, as the golden rule of the Government Car Service was that you never left the airport until the plane was in the air. The hostess in charge of the VIP suite said, "Would you like a cup of coffee while you are waiting?" I said, "That would be very nice, thank you." As she began making the drink, the teleprinter came on and when she glanced at it she said, "Oh my God, they have just shut down the airport!"

About fifteen minutes later, the cars arrived back from the plane with their passengers and, as they walked into the VIP suite, Sir Geoffrey said to me, "I'm glad you're still here". But he added, "Where are all the other drivers?" I said, "As soon as you got in the cars, they all left including the Governor of the Bank of England's driver." The Governor was left with little option other than to stay in the Gatwick hotel overnight. But we were to find out later that he was without his cheque-book, acceptable credit card or sufficient cash for the occasion. But luckily, they did agree to let him stay. As Sir Geoffrey said, "It's good to know that even central bank governors are sometimes brought down to earth."

I was then approached by Sir Geoffrey and John Kerr, who asked me what I thought the chances were of being able to drive them to the Dover ferry terminal. I said that I wasn't sure but I would give it a go and I had a full tank of petrol. As we were about to leave, one of the policeman in the VIP suite said," Good luck. I believe the road is already blocked where you join the motorway". So began one of the most memorable journeys in my 46 years' experience as a GCS driver.

Fortunately, Lady Luck seemed to be with us all the way. Our first slice of luck happened as we were going up a hill where all the lorries had jack-knifed, blocking the road. Luckily there was one gap in the crash-barrier, where I was able to squeeze through and cross onto the other side of the carriageway, where there was no traffic at all. When we eventually arrived at Canterbury, all the road signs were unreadable because they were covered in snow. But somehow we managed to find the right way through. Our final hurdle was on the cliff-top highway, just short of Dover, where the road was completely blocked by six or eight feet of snow. Out of the gloom appeared a policeman with a lantern, who said, "You won't be able to go any further. The road is completely blocked". I said to Sir Geoffrey, "It's four miles to Dover ahead or sixty five miles back the way we came."

As we sat there pondering what to do, we noticed out of the right hand side window of the car, some flashing orange lights. John Kerr put the side window down to get a better look and realised that it was a snow plough. He immediately got out of our car and went over to the snow plough driver and told him who we were. He asked him if he would be kind enough to cut a hole through the snow drifts so we could get through. It was one of those machines that blew the snow to one side. He agreed to try and said, "I'll have a go. Just follow me."

It took about ten minutes to get through and then the road was manageable to drive on. As we got to the outskirts of Dover town, Sir Geoffrey turned on the radio to listen to the 10 o'clock News. We were amazed to hear that it had been reported that Sir Geoffrey Howe was stuck in a snow drift just outside Dover. We assumed that it must have been the snow plough driver who had reported the incident to his office and they had told the news programme.

We drove straight onto the ferry, which was just about to leave. Sir Geoffrey and John Kerr got out of the car and I drove off the ferry, which then departed for France. Our journey had taken ten hours in all. I managed to find somewhere to stay in Dover overnight and left next morning to go home.

Another memorable incident took place in November 1982 when Sir Geoffrey was returning to London from Manchester and was travelling in an overnight sleeping carriage. He admitted that he was foolish to forget to lock the door of his compartment and unfortunately had his trousers stolen. The thief had taken £100 cash and threw the trousers out of the train, near Nuneaton, where they were eventually recovered and returned to Sir Geoffrey at No. 11 Downing Street. It was reported in the paper that his driver/bodyguard, Peter Smithson, had ticked him off about the incident. This proves that you can't believe everything you read in the newspapers, because I was not his bodyguard, nor did I tell him off. The cartoonists had a field day with illustrations of Sir Geoffrey standing in his pants at a railway station, and so on. Even radio Moscow reported the disaster and Pravda made a meal of it. But fortunately, Sir Geoffrey had a spare pair of trousers with him and was able to emerge from an embarrassing situation with honour.

Sir Geoffrey was always an excellent passenger to have in the car. Not only was he unperturbed by any bad road conditions or occasions when high speed through traffic was required, but he was also very helpful to his driver. When he was Chancellor, and before we had Special Branch protection, Sir Geoffrey would always get hold of the map when we were going on a long journey to a small town or village (there was no satellite navigation in those days) and navigate us safely to our destination. I knew he enjoyed doing this and so it got to the point that when he got into the car, I just used a hand him the map and off we went.

Looking back now, it seems strange how Ministers without police protection had to look out for themselves in many situations. For example, I remember one occasion when Sir Geoffrey had an invitation to the launch of a Sunday newspaper colour supplement. It was to be held in the Whitbread Brewery building in Chiswell St. near the Barbican. We parked inside the courtyard and Sir Geoffrey said to me, "It's a buffet lunch, so come in with us and get your meal as well."

We walked into a large ground floor building, which had a long table down one side of the room, full of all kinds of food and there were plenty of tables and chairs to be seated. On his entry, Sir Geoffrey was greeted by a group of gentlemen, so I wandered off and had a look around to see if there was anyone there I knew. Soon afterwards, Sir Geoffrey went over to the buffet table, put some food on his plate and took a seat. I noticed that he had been joined by the famous comedian, Frankie Howard.

I walked over to the buffet table and started to put some food onto my plate. As I was examining the large selection on offer, I noticed that the woman standing next to me filling her plate was the infamous Cynthia Payne, otherwise known as 'Miss Whiplash!' I recognised her immediately as she had recently been in the news for running a house of ill repute. She turned to me and said, "Hello." But before I could answer, a man who was obviously a photographer came up to her and said, "Cynthia, I've got a good photo shot if you are interested." He then pointed to Sir Geoffrey and Frankie Howard, who were having their lunch and said to her, "I want you to go up behind them, put your arms around them and your head in between and give me a big smile and I'll take the photo." She smiled and said, "Okay."

I put my plate down and went straight over to Sir Geoffrey and told him what they were planning. Sir Geoffrey immediately stood up and said to Frankie Howard, "I'm going to get a coffee." Afterwards he walked over to another gentleman who he seemed to know quite well and started chatting to him. When we got back into the car, Sir Geoffrey thanked me for being alert to a situation which could have resulted in an embarrassing photograph in the newspapers.

Talking of embarrassing photographs, I am reminded of an incident that took place in March 1982 when we all emerged from No 11 Downing St. to the sound of people cheering and cameras clicking as Sir Geoffrey was leaving to present his budget to the House of Commons. I went over to the driver's side of the car, whilst Lady Howe stood next to Sir Geoffrey as he held up his red budget box for the assembled photographers. One of these who was standing close to them shouted,

"Take some photos," to Lady Howe, who was holding her small Agfamatic camera by her side. To please him, she happily complied and simply held up the camera and without any deliberation, quickly pressed the shutter a few times and took a few random shots. One of the pressmen then asked if they could develop the film and Lady Howe replied, "Yes, so long as you don't print anything without letting me vet it first."

The next day, we were all shocked to see a whole page of the *Daily Express* newspaper devoted to some of her fuzzy and out of focus snaps, one of which included me standing by the official car, with the headline "Howe not to take a picture" complete with a professional critique. Although neither Sir Geoffrey nor Lady Howe made a fuss about their ill-manners, I was very annoyed by the impertinence of the newspaper, as they were both very keen photographers, who were well known to take excellent photos.

In April 1983 Sir Geoffrey and Lady Howe were invited to the Royal Mint, which was situated on a site opposite the Tower of London, and asked to strike the first one pound coin. They kindly invited me in with them and I watched as Lady Howe pushed the button and the first coin was stamped out. It was soon afterwards that the one pound note was taken out of circulation and the one pound coin was introduced to replace it and the Royal Mint was moved to Wales.

In all my time with Sir Geoffrey while he was Chancellor of the Exchequer, I only lobbied him on two issues regarding his budgets. The first concerned the tax treatment of mortgage interest relief available at that time for the first £25,000 borrowed on your principal residence This ceiling on mortgage interest rate seemed unfairly low to me and I complained that although it wasn't so long ago that you could buy a whole estate for £25,000, the situation was now very different. For example, I bought my first house in 1956 for £1,900. But within two years you would have had to pay £4,000 for the same house. So, house prices were going up so quickly that the £25,000 ceiling meant very little. And I thought it only fair that the rate of tax relief should have increased at the same pace. Unfortunately, Sir Geoffrey was not of the same opinion, as he said in his memoirs,

"The only contrary argument which came near to persuading me had come... (he acknowledged that it was the only time he had ever been lobbied by me) from Peter Smithson, my driver: '£25,000', he said, 'would have bought a small country estate in the year when I first joined the Car Service.'

But Sir Geoffrey was unmoved and added that he told Margaret Thatcher that neither he nor his Treasury ministers thought it was the right thing to do to raise the ceiling. In fact Margaret Thatcher herself wanted to raise the ceiling to £35,000 but after much discussion. Sir Geoffrey decided to split the difference at £30,000.

Later on I did lobby Sir Geoffrey over another issue, which was taken up at a later date. It concerned the vehicle road tax that was at that time levied on classic cars as well as more modern vehicles. I said that it was a bit unfair to pay tax on an old classic car as most of them were kept off the road and did very little mileage. Eventually cars registered before 1972 would become exempt from Road Tax.

I was particularly interested in this subject because during the whole of the time I was in the GCS, my main hobby had been classic cars. I have always enjoyed working on these cars to restore them as well as having one to drive. One of the first cars I bought for restoration was an MG Magnette. Once I had rebuilt it, I joined the MG Car Club, where my ambition was to win the concours event. After a lot of hard work, I was very pleased to achieve the coveted first prize on my second attempt. I soon realised that there was a lot of interest in classic British cars, so my next ambition was to own a classic Jaguar sports car.

On one occasion when I was parked up in London, I got talking to a couple of tourists from the USA and we got round to the subject of classic cars. They told me that the best place to get a British classic car was in the USA. I knew that just after Second World War, 90% of British sports cars were exported there, as we were desperate for cash and needed to get our exports moving. In Britain it had become very hard to find British classic sports cars and the prices they were fetching were very high.

Later, I discussed this matter with two of my sons Kevin and Neil and we decided to take a trip to Florida. So I took two weeks annual leave and off we went hoping to pick up a bargain. We flew to Miami as a base and bought a magazine called 'The Trader', which covered Florida for cars, especially classic cars. However, the problem was, Florida is such a big place that it was not unusual to find the car we wanted to see could be 600 miles away. We looked at quite a few on our way travelling north, but it was sometimes disappointing to find, for example, that a very nice British sports car had been fitted with an American engine. That wasn't what we wanted.

However, by our second week we had bought a very nice MG near Miami. In addition there was also a very nice E-type Jaguar for sale, which we wanted to see but unfortunately this was in Tampa, about 600 miles away. So off we went and on our arrival found a beautiful car exactly what we wanted. As we only had two days left of our holiday before we flew back home again, we paid for it in cash and decided to drive it back overnight to Miami. The problem was that once we started on our journey, I discovered that there were hardly any brakes, which meant I could only break by using the gears. Fortunately as it was nearly 95% motorway to Miami, I didn't have to use the brakes very much anyway!

We left as soon as we could in the evening and I drove the car all night. However, we arrived in Miami just as the rush-hour had started, which was a bit hairy to say the least. Nevertheless, we managed to deliver the car safely to our agent, who was going to ship it back to England with the MG. The cars eventually arrived back in England with no problems and we were pleased with both cars.

14 AMBITION ACHIEVED - DRIVING SIR GEOFFREY HOWE (FOREIGN SECRETARY)

At the reshuffle in June 1983, Sir Geoffrey was given the prestigious post of Foreign Secretary. I remember arriving at No. 11 on that morning and going in to see him in his office to congratulate him on his new post. It so happened that it was the job I had always aspired to, as it had been the practice for the Foreign Secretary's driver to go on overseas visits with him as the Baggage Master. As I walked into his office, I was surprised to see a Superintendent from Special Branch having a chat with Sir Geoffrey. The Superintendent made it quite clear from the start that he thought the police should now take over the driving of the Foreign Secretary because he would then have full-time police protection. In the ensuing conversation, I was quick to explain to the officer that the Prime Minister was driven by the GCS and I could not see any reason for changing the system for the Foreign Secretary. In addition, I emphasized that I had waited many years to get this particular job that I had always coveted and I had no intention now of giving it up easily by standing aside.

The Police Superintendent insisted that the police drivers were far more experienced and professional, having been on the anti-terrorist course at Hendon Police Training School. But I then pointed out to him that the GCS used to drive the Home Secretary, as I myself had done on many occasions when I had been in the pool and was asked to stand in for his driver, but the police had then insisted that they take over that job. I went on to remind him that soon after the police had taken over this responsibility, the Home Secretary's car had been stolen from outside Scotland Yard! This to my knowledge was a first. The GCS had never lost a car, nor had one stolen, as far as I knew. I reiterated that the Prime Minister was also being driven by the GCS without any problems. Needless to say, the Superintendent eventually agreed, with the proviso that I should take and pass the specialist police advanced driving and anti-terrorist course at Hendon. I agreed because of the increased threat that existed at that time, and was relieved that I could continue to stay on the job as the Foreign Secretary's driver.

On 29 November 1983, I received a letter from number 10 Downing Street to inform me that the Queen had approved the Prime Minister's recommendation for me to be awarded the British Empire Medal (BEM), which was to be announced in the New Year's Honours list. I felt very honoured and told Sir Geoffrey about the award. He said he would like to be the one to present it to me. However, as he had a very busy schedule, it took quite some time before he had the opportunity for the presentation, which was eventually held in the Foreign Office. This turned out to be one of the most memorable occasions in my career. Later, on leaving the GCS, I would receive a letter on 15 October 2003 from the Central Chancellery of the Orders of Knighthood, St James's Palace, to say that her Majesty the Queen had been graciously pleased to award me with the Imperial Service Medal for meritorious service. When I started to work for the GCS at the age of 23, I never imagined that I would be there for 47 years, with only approximately six weeks off sick, let alone to achieve any of these honours.

15 TRIALS AND TRIBULATIONS IN MIAMI

The following year, I took two weeks leave and flew out to Florida again with my two sons as we were looking for a couple of Jaguar XK sports cars. At this time it was becoming more difficult to find British sports cars, as there seemed to be lots of 'Brits' doing the same thing, because the prices were going sky high. I remember that on one occasion, we went to look at a car that was deep in the Everglades along very narrow tracks and swampy land, well off the beaten track. Eventually we came to a clearing that looked like one of those hillbilly films. There was the old boy, sitting on the veranda smoking his pipe. We asked if this was where the car was for sale, to which he answered, 'Yep' and pointed to a lean to, with a British Sunbeam Tiger car in it. I noticed what looked like a bullet hole in the windscreen on the driver's side. So I asked the old boy, if it was a bullet hole and he just smiled and said, 'Yep'. We decided that this was perhaps not the car for us! We said our goodbyes and as we were leaving another car drew up and another couple of Brits got out and were asking about the car. No matter where you went to look at a car, another 'Brit' seemed to turn up and therefore the prices were starting to rise.

The day before we were due to leave Miami to come home, a friend of ours called Scottie, who worked for our car shipper, telephoned to tell us about a very nice E-type for sale. As it was close by, we decided to go and have a look at it. It was a very nice car but as we had bought a car the day before and only had $3000 left, and the car cost $23,000, we said we would like to buy it but didn't have enough cash with us to buy it outright. We came to an agreement to buy the car by leaving a deposit of $3000 and would send him the balance through our shipping agent. So we did the deal and went to our agent, Ron Gandhi, to tell him. He agreed he would do the deal for us and ship the car straight away, once we had paid for it.

We arrived back in England the next day and made the arrangements to send $20,000 to our agent. A week later, as we hadn't heard anything, I rang our agent but got no answer. The next day I tried again. This time, my friend Scotty answered the phone. I asked him what was the progress with the car I had bought, and he said, "Peter get yourself out here. He's going to rip you off." So I immediately went to see Sir Geoffrey and told him I needed to have a week's leave straight away and explained why. He agreed to this.

I flew out to Miami the next day and was picked up by another friend I knew there, who drove me to my shipper's office. I went inside, where Ron Gandhi was sitting with three of his staff. I could tell he was quite surprised to see me. He said he was just about to leave to go to a big car auction. I said, "I'm not interested in the auction. I've come to see about the car I bought from you." He said, "Come back to see me tomorrow". I said, "I've just flown all the way From England. No way am I leaving it 'till tomorrow. Let's get it sorted out now." At this point, he opened his briefcase, which was on the desk in front of him and took out a chrome plated 45 automatic. He cocked it and said, "Get out of here now or I'll blow your effing head off!"

At this my friend, who had taken me there, ran out of the office. I said to Ron Gandhi, "Are you really trying to tell me you would shoot me in front of three witnesses, and all for $23,000?" He put the gun back in the briefcase and said, "Come back tomorrow and I'll give you your money." He then made some kind of excuse, saying he did not think the car was worth the money. Then Ron Gandhi went outside, jumped into his car and drove off.

So I decided to go to the local police headquarters at Fort Lauderdale and ask them to look into the situation. The detectives in charge said, "I have a long list of Brits getting ripped off, so go back tomorrow as he asked you and if he doesn't give you your money, come back and see me." I did go back the following day, but everything was locked up. However, as I had Scottie's telephone number, I rang him at home and he said that Ron Gandhi would be in his office in two days time. He also gave me the name of a man who, he said, could get me the cash back for 25% of the money recovered. But when I rang this man to ask how he would go about getting my money back, he replied that he would drive past his house and shoot a few rounds into it, or maybe nail his dog to the front door. I said, "I'll think about that one!"

That evening, I telephoned Sir Geoffrey to let him know how I was getting on. I told him that I thought the police didn't seem very interested as they said they had a large pile of cases of Brits getting ripped off. Sir Geoffrey then gave me the telephone number of one of his American friends, called George Smith who I had met in London when he had visited Sir Geoffrey and said I could ring him and ask his advice. So I rang him and he answered, saying he couldn't talk very much as he was cruising in his yacht in the Caribbean. However, he told me that he would give me the telephone number of his friend at Miami FBI headquarters. He would also give them a call to let them know that I was coming. I telephoned the FBI the next day and they seemed to be expecting my call as they asked me to go along that afternoon.

When I arrived at the headquarters, it was a very imposing and obviously secure building. I gave my name and, as they were obviously expecting me, I was immediately escorted in and taken to an office where the man behind the desk seemed to be the top man in charge. I told him the full story and he said he would do what he could to help. He continued that he would get in touch with Fort Lauderdale police headquarters and tell them to look into the case. He asked me a bit about my job back home and seemed very interested. I was also given a letter by him to hand into the police headquarters. He said he would make an appointment for me at 10 o'clock the next day.

The following day I made sure I arrived there nice and early and this time the detectives seemed very keen to help. The detective in charge explained that he needed me to go back to Ron Gandhi's office and confront him again. He asked if I was prepared to be fitted with a wire as they needed hard evidence and wanted me to get as much information out of him as I could. I happily agreed to this and the police fitted me up with the wire.

Next morning I got to Ron Gandhi's office early, just after he had arrived. As I walked in, he was sitting at his desk talking to two of his staff. He looked up and said to me, "Not you again," and I answered, "Yes it's me and I'm not leaving this time without the money you owe me." I knew I had to get him to give the right answers and the information needed by the police. So I said to him, "You pulled a gun on me yesterday and threatened to blow my head off." He said, "Yes, F... off or I'll blow your head off right now." At this he opened his briefcase and took out his gun again. I said to him, "You didn't just take the $20,000 I sent to you to buy the car but you even went back to the man selling the car, made an excuse, and said I wanted the deposit back and stole that as well. So you owe me $23,000." I continued by telling him that I had made enquiries with a lawyer and they said that stealing more than $11,000 was a federal offence.

On hearing this, he got out of his chair swearing and started throwing things around the room. Both of his staff now got up and walked out. I realised that I had got all the information I needed and I thought it was now time to get out quickly. I left and went round the corner to the next block, where the police were waiting for me to take me back to Fort Lauderdale headquarters. Once inside, they removed the wire and the tape recorder and played it back. They seemed pleased with the result and said yes, it was exactly what they needed. Straightaway, they drove back to his office and arrested him.

I was then advised by the detective to get myself a lawyer as there would obviously be a court case. This I did and managed to find a lady lawyer who was very keen to deal with the case. Soon afterwards I went back to my hotel in Miami as I wasn't sure how long I would have to stay in Florida. I was due to leave on Saturday, but on the Friday morning I had a telephone call to my room in the hotel, asking me if I would now do the deposition over the telephone against Ron Gandhi. I agreed but explained that we were in the middle of quite a bad storm, and it was going to be a bit noisy.

I had been on the telephone for about five minutes, when I said, "Good God" out loud. My lawyer said, "Are you alright?" I answered, "Yes but I'm on the second floor and a palm tree has just gone past my window!" She asked if I was sure I was okay and I said, "Yes" and carried on talking. About five minutes later, there was a terrific crashing noise and the lawyer said, "What was that?" I said, "You're not going to believe this, but the whole roof has just come off the hotel and is now in the river!" Sounding rather worried, she asked again, "Are you sure you alright?" I assured her that I was fine, but she said, "I think we've got all we want, so let's call it a day!" I put the telephone down and ran outside, to be confronted with what looked like an absolute disaster zone. However, the storm suddenly subsided and I started to look for somewhere else to stay before returning home to England to wait for the court case to come round.

About four weeks later, I had a telephone call from America to let me know that the trial of Ron Gandhi would be in about a week's time. So once again, I took leave and flew out to Fort Lauderdale. I immediately went to see my lawyer, who told me that there were two other people who had lost their money to Ron Gandhi and they would also be in court and the case would be held in two days time. She was a first-class lawyer and went over all the important points with me.

On the day of the trial, we went into the court room and Gandhi arrived shortly afterwards. The judge came in and the trial started. I was surprised that Ron Gandhi tried to say that the whole case was a misunderstanding. But once the tape of our meeting, with him threatening me with the gun, was played to the court, Gandhi realised that the game was lost. The judge seemed very angry with him and the trial was over very quickly and he was found guilty.

Ron Gandhi was obviously afraid of going to prison because he weighed about 18 stone and the police told me he wouldn't last five minutes if he finished up on the chain gang. So he asked the judge whether he could go on probation if he paid back all the money he owed me. The judge then called me to his bench and said, "What you really want is your money back, isn't it?" I replied, "Yes." The judge turned to Ron Gandhi and said, "I will put you on probation, on condition that you pay Mr Smithson all his money back plus expenses and you are not allowed to leave the State." Ron Gandhi said that he did not have all the money, but would pay me $3000 immediately and the rest at $1000 a month. I said I agreed, provided he also paid the interest on the money he owed me, plus my expenses. The judge warned Gandhi that he must play fair because if he missed a payment he would be arrested.

The court then went into recess and the judge asked if I would join him in his chambers. My lawyer looked at me in surprise and said, "I've never seen that happen before." Once inside, the judge invited me to take a seat and began to ask me about my job in England. He also seemed to be very proud that he was descended from English stock. I told him that I was the official driver of the Foreign Secretary. He then went on to ask if I had ever met Mrs Thatcher, who he seemed to admire. I said yes, I knew her quite well before she was Prime Minister and that her present driver, Denis Oliver, was a good friend of mine, who had also been in the RAF. We had a very friendly chat for about 20 minutes and then I said my goodbyes. When I went out to my lawyer, she said she was amazed that I had been invited into his chambers because that was most unusual and she seemed very impressed.

Soon afterwards, I got my first $3000 paid through my lawyer and thereafter received $1000 a month for about six months and then, surprisingly, I had a cheque sent to me for the full outstanding amount to close the case.

Amongst other cars brought from America, I now had three Jaguar sports cars; an XK120, XK140 and an XK150 that were badly in need of restoration. Together with my son Kevin, who had served his apprenticeship at Jaguar in the body shop and rebuilds and become a first rate restorer, we rebuilt all three cars over the next few years. Eventually, we sold two of them but I kept my favourite XK120 OTS (open top sports), which I was to enjoy driving over the next twenty years.

Meanwhile, I was continuing my demanding but enjoyable job as driver for the Foreign Secretary. I had managed to put off taking the advanced driving and ant-terrorist course at Hendon Police College for quite a long time, as I didn't think it was necessary since most of the security issues were down to commonsense. In any case we had received our own excellent 'in-house-training'. Drivers in the GCS had been shown many films on how to avoid terrorist attacks. In addition, we would have a team of first class police protection officers working with us and one of their officers would be with us at all times.

However, one morning, when Sir Geoffrey came out from a meeting at No.10, he told me that he would soon be going on an overseas trip for about two weeks. He suggested that it might be a good time for me to go on the Hendon course and get it over with. I thought that this seemed a good idea and arranged to go on the course.

So I went along to attend the advanced driving and anti-terrorist course, which lasted from 3rd to 14th September 1984. When I arrived, I found that the police instructors were indeed very professional. In the first part of the course we were shown films of what to do in emergencies. One example was how to ram a car in an attempted hijacking by driving into the rear of the car rather than the front, which would be heavier because of the engine. This would have the effect of spinning it out of the way and you could continue your journey without stopping. We were also told that if our car was stopped by hijackers, they would usually try to shoot the driver first and then help themselves to the passengers!

On about the fourth day, we started the practical part of the course, our driving tests. Every morning our police instructor would pick up three drivers and off we would go driving for many miles. Each person on the course would take it in turn to drive the car. The police instructor would push the driver to go very fast, who at the same time had to give a running commentary on what they were approaching during the journey. I took my turn second and after driving for about an hour, I was told to pull in to a lay-by and then the third driver, a lady, took over.

This was when I had one of the most hair raising drives of my life. The lady should never have been on the course, although she was an excellent driver under normal conditions. But when she was being pushed at high speed, she became very nervous and disorientated. The worst incident of her drive took place when we joined the motorway for our return to Hendon. We were travelling at 70 miles an hour in the fast lane. The car we were in was an unmarked police car, but the police instructor with us was in full police uniform, although not wearing his hat. A large Mercedes was close behind us and kept flashing his headlights for us to pull over and let him pass. As there was very heavy traffic at the time we were unable to do this. The Mercedes driver then managed to pull alongside us in the middle lane. He then started blowing his horn and making rude gestures with two fingers. With this, the police instructor put on his hat and held up a large sign which read 'POLICE'. On seeing this, the Mercedes driver seemed to panic and slightly lose control of his vehicle. In doing so, he just clipped the rear of our car. This made our lady driver swerve and bounce off the steel centre barrier, and all this at about 70 miles an hour!

Our police instructor signalled to the Mercedes driver to pull over and we finished up coming to a stop on the hard shoulder, where our police officer got out of the car and gave the Mercedes driver a dressing down and took his particulars as there was quite a lot of damage to the side of our car. Our lady driver was in no fit state to carry on to Hendon so the police officer took over.

The next day we went onto the skid pan where you had to drive a car with bald tyres on an area covered with oil and water. The object was to negotiate around bollards without losing control of your car. It seemed very difficult at first, but once the instructor showed you how to do it, then it was not too hard.

Eventually the course came to an end and we were invited into a hall where I, together with others, were presented with a certificate confirming that we had passed all aspects of the course. The lady driver, who had nearly killed us, was of course notable by her absence having quickly decided to call it a day.

When Sir Geoffrey returned from his overseas trip, I picked him up from the airport. He immediately enquired how I had got on at Hendon. I told him that it had been very interesting and that the police instructors were very impressive. Although I hadn't been too keen to go on the course at first, I must admit that I was glad to have done it as it was to come in very useful, especially when I was told later that the IRA had intended to kill Sir Geoffrey by blowing him up or attacking him in his car.

A few days later, I was informed that as the risk factor was now very high against Sir Geoffrey I would be getting a new up-rated armoured car. So one morning, the following week, I was asked to go down to the Foreign Office courtyard where I was to have a look at my new car which had just been delivered. When I went up to the car, which was a Jaguar, I noticed that there were quite few people there already, including Sir Geoffrey. The delivery driver then started a demonstration to show us over the car.

The gentleman who delivered the car to us was very keen to show us all the special equipment that was fitted. After he'd finished his demonstration, he asked if there were any questions. So, Sir Geoffrey said to me," You will be the one driving it, so, what is your opinion of it?" I opened the door and sat in the driver's seat, noticing that the front door was very heavy. The first thing I saw was a 3 inch long aluminium tube next to the rear view mirror. I asked what it was and received the reply that it was a fire extinguisher. He went on to explain that if there was a fire in the car it would fill the car with foam in a few seconds. I said I didn't think that this was a very good system because if it went off accidentally whilst we were travelling, it would be a disaster. He then continued that if we were attacked by gas, there were gas masks in the car, one under each of the two front seats and two in the back of the front seats for the rear passengers. So I then attempted to get the gas mask that was under my front seat to try it on, but was unable to get it out as there was very little room in the foot well. So the only way to get the gas mask out from under the seat was to open the door and get out of the car, pull the gas mask from under the seat, put it on, and then get back into the car. This I thought defeated the whole object of the exercise! I also found that the armoured door was so heavy that it was hard to hold the door open and get out of the car if you were on an incline.

I then went round to the rear of the car to have a look at the boot, which I was told was not armoured. When I opened it. I noticed that there were four large cylinders at the back of the boot. I was told by the demonstrator that they were the oxygen cylinders for supplying air to the gas masks. This didn't impress me one little bit, as I explained that if one bullet went into the rear of the car and hit a cylinder, the car could go up like a bomb.

Following this demonstration, the car was taken back to the depot, where the fire extinguisher, gas masks and rear cylinders in the boot were removed. Then the car was delivered back to us. This Jaguar served us for quite a long time. The only problem we had with it was that although it went very fast, because it was so heavy it was difficult to stop at speed. To show how heavy the car was, it had a two ton trolley jack in the boot, which I took out one day in order to change a punctured rear tyre. I had started pumping up the jack when I noticed that the car wasn't lifting. I looked under the car and saw that it was because the jack was sinking into the road, due to the car's weight. The tyre was eventually changed with the help of a breakdown vehicle.

While I had been at Hendon, the police instructors had explained that one of the main threats we must look out for were motorcyclists who, if given the opportunity, would come alongside the car and attempt to slap a magnetic mine to the roof. We were told that we would only have a few seconds to stop the car and get out before the mine exploded and punched a hole in the car and possibly kill everybody inside. Unfortunately, to be able to stop the car and get out in these few seconds would be practically impossible. Therefore, we were told we must never give a motorcyclist the opportunity to get that close to us. These words were to come back to haunt me at a later date.

16 THE BRIGHTON BOMB

However, at this time another important event intervened that was to have dramatic and long lasting effects on many people. It was October 1984 and one of the most interesting occasions that all ministers' drivers looked forward to very much was approaching - the party conferences. These were usually held at Bournemouth, Blackpool or Brighton and it was always a very hectic time from early morning to late at night.

The Conservative party conference that year was held at Brighton and it was a very intense experience as the IRA was very active at that time. Whenever we left our accommodation at the 'Grand Hotel' to go to the conference centre, we had police escorts and very rarely went the same route twice, as the police were very careful and professional with their organised routes to the conference centre.

Usually the Prime Minister's car and the Foreign Secretary's car parked either side of the main front door of the hotel and a police constable would keep an eye on them twenty four hours of the day. But on this particular occasion we were told to take our cars around to the back of the hotel into an area where all the police vehicles and men were together. I thought this was a good idea, as anyone passing the hotel would not know whether the Prime Minister or the Foreign Secretary, were there or not.

I remember on the fateful evening of the bomb explosion that I went out of the front door of the 'Grand Hotel' and said to the police constable on duty. "Here we are in October and it's a very warm night". I continued to say that I was waiting for the Prime Minister to return because her driver, Denis Oliver, was a good friend of mine and we had arranged to have a night-cap once we were both off duty. The P.C. said, "I think you need to go to the rear of the hotel as she will be dropped off there." So I duly made my way round to the rear car park.

Just as I arrived I saw my friend Denis, Mrs Thatcher's driver, getting out of his car. I greeted him, and we walked through to the bar area. As we arrived, we noticed that the staff were pulling down the bar shutters and when we walked up to them they said, "Sorry, the bar is shut." Denis turned to me and said, "I can't believe it. They were still serving drinks at midnight last night, and it's only 10.45." We sat down and had a little chat about what we've been doing before saying our good nights.

I had a room in the annex at the back of the hotel and as we had an early start the next morning I went straight to bed and immediately dropped off to sleep. The next thing I remember was somebody banging on the bedroom door. I jumped out of bed and opened the door to see one of our protection officers who said, "Quick, get some clothes on. A bomb has gone off in the main building."

I hurriedly pulled on some clothes and we both ran to the front of the hotel. It was very hard to see as a lot of the lights were out and the building was full of dust. I think it was just the emergency lighting that had come on. We struggled past debris and ran up the main staircase to where the hotel suites were situated. As we approached the entrance to Sir Geoffrey and Lady Howe's suite, I saw that the door had disappeared and what used to be his sitting-room was just a black hole. As I peered inside my heart sank, as through the black dust I could see down at least two floors. Almost immediately, a police officer approached us and asked if we were Sir Geoffrey's team. When the Special Branch officer said, "Yes", he continued that they were both alright and had been taken away to a safe house out of the danger area. At this stage it was not known whether there were any more bombs in the 'Grand'. So, we immediately turned around and ran back down the staircase, finding our way through the black dust and past many people who were rushing about in the debris, towards the back exit. (The front entrance of the hotel had disappeared with the explosion). We reached our car and were told to follow a waiting police motorcyclist.

When we arrived at the safe house, we went straight inside and were very relieved to see Lady Howe and Sir Geoffrey and also my little friend, their Jack Russell dog 'Summit', all unhurt. It was decided that they should go on and spend the rest of the night at Chevening, as it was only about 50 miles away and nearly all motorway along the M23 and M25. Once we were in our car, we joined a high-speed police convoy that swept us there in time for a short rest. However, there was not much time to take a breather, because it had been decided by the Prime Minister, Sir Geoffrey and other senior ministers that the conference would go ahead as usual the next morning.

So after breakfast we left Chevening and were back at the conference centre for the normal morning start. Without further eventualities the conference ended and we were ready to leave. It was then that I had another of the most hair-raising drives of my life. I was told afterwards that the police were worried that the IRA would try to catch senior ministers in their cars as they went from the conference centre and through Brighton, and even possibly onto the motorways. I had two police motorcyclists with me, who went ahead to stop traffic at the traffic lights and main junctions so we could drive straight through at speed. I also had a car in front of me and one behind with four men in each one. Before we left the conference centre, one of the men from the front car had said to me, "When you leave, keep very close to me at all times." At this time, I was not quite sure where we going or by what route.

So we left Brighton and very soon went onto a dual carriageway and then onto a motorway. I was looking at the motorway signs to see where we were heading, but then we would suddenly go off in a different direction. The Special Branch officer sitting next to me had a walkie-talkie and was in touch with the lead car. Eventually after answering one call he turned to me and said, "We are going to Sir Geoffrey's Warwickshire home."

Once we got onto the motorway again, I noticed that our two police motorcyclists were giving us a wave and then they left us at the next exit. Then about halfway home we parted company with the back-up car, although the lead car still kept with us, travelling at a very fast pace and constantly reminding us to keep up close. Sir Geoffrey was his usual relaxed self and doing what he always did, reading the newspapers or working on his official papers.

Eventually we arrived at his home in Warwickshire and pulled up outside his house. Sir Geoffrey got out of our car and went up to the lead car to thank the occupants and shake their hands. As he approached their car, they all got out and I could see that they were all very fit looking young men. After thanking them Sir Geoffrey turned to me and said, "Peter take them down to the village pub and get them a meal and whatever they want and it's on me." It soon became obvious to our protection officer and me that they were special service men and I was told at a later date that they were S.A.S. So we all went down to the pub to have a good meal and chat and I felt very honoured and proud to have been in their company.

Two days later I went back to Brighton to the 'Grand Hotel' with one of the protection officers. We had been told that workers who were clearing the rubble had found Lady Howe's handbag and Sir Geoffrey's official box about two floors down from their suite. As we were walking back to our car at the rear of the hotel, I noticed some skips with lots of rubble and other bits and pieces in them. A conference poster of the government caught my eye. So I asked the man who seemed to be in charge if I could have the framed poster as a keepsake. He said, "Help yourself; it's all just going to be dumped." I still have the framed print today. Later on, I was told that the bomb had been hidden under a bath on the top floor, which was directly over the sitting rooms of the suites below. If the bomb had been two rooms along on the top floor, it would have taken out the bedrooms below and most of the cabinet with it.

17 LIVING WITH THE I.R.A. THREAT

During the period of time following this incident, the IRA continued to be very threatening and active, which meant we had to be extremely vigilant and careful. One Sunday evening as we were returning to London, we left Sir Geoffrey's Warwickshire home and drove out onto the adjacent main road, where we were soon joined by two motorcyclists following behind us, who were dressed completely in black, including their helmets and visors. On this occasion I was accompanied by a Special Branch officer who was really on the ball. He said, "Have you noticed the two motorcyclists behind us?" and I replied, "Yes, I have." After about a mile, during which time I was changing my driving speed from very fast to quite slow to give them the opportunity to overtake me, they continued to follow closely behind us. Thoughts of my recent Hendon, anti-terrorist training course kept coming into my head. They had clearly told us that our main concern regarding terrorists should be motorcyclists, as they could quite easily clamp a magnetic bomb onto the roof of your car, if you let them get close enough.

By now, the Special Branch officer and I had started to get a bit concerned. He said to me, "You know about a mile further on down this road, there's a turning off to the left that we sometimes take?" I said quietly. "Yes, I'll go that way." It was a small, narrow B road but it was a good way to get to the motorway with hardly any traffic. We arrived at the road and turned into it, fully expecting to lose our motorcyclists if they stayed on the main road. Unfortunately, they turned off the main road as well and continued to ride behind us. Now the Special Branch officer was getting very concerned and said to me, "When we get to the next village, you know where we go down a steep road and at the bottom of the hill there is a sharp right-hand turn but also a small road that goes straight ahead into a dead-end?" I nodded. "Well go down the hill and into the dead-end and then stop immediately. I'll jump out there and deal with them."

I must admit that by now I was getting very anxious, because this appeared to be a very dangerous situation and everything was happening so quickly. As we got to the bottom of the hill, I went straight ahead as agreed and the Special Branch officer was out of the car before it stopped. However, to our relief, the motorcyclists had turned off right and were continuing on their way.

Whilst all this was happening, Sir Geoffrey had been engrossed in his work and had said nothing. But as we pulled up in the dead-end, he looked up and said "Why have we stopped here?" I just replied. "Sorry sir, I took the wrong turn," as I started to back the car up and continued on our way to London. I often wondered what would have happened if the motorcyclists had indeed followed us up into the dead-end!

One weekend, Sir Geoffrey and Lady Howe were invited to a wedding of a close friend in the City of London. Later that day, there was to be a reception at 'La Residence' restaurant in Bayswater Road on the corner of Holland Park Avenue. When we arrived for the reception, Sir Geoffrey said to me, "Park the car Peter. You have been invited in for a meal." As the risk factor was very high at the time, there were also two armed Special Branch officers on duty that day and they were to be automatically seated close to Sir Geoffrey and Lady Howe. The police officer who was on duty had made arrangements for me to park our car just on the corner side of the restaurant, which was on the corner of the main road and a side street. He had also arranged for a police car to drive around the area and keep an eye on our car. The main party, including Education Secretary, Kenneth Baker, were nearly all seated in the lower basement, which had been turned into a function room. The party went very well and I made a point of going out to check on the car every so often.

I think it was about 10 o'clock, when Sir Geoffrey came over to us and said, "We'll be leaving in a short time." So, I said to the Police Superintendent in charge, "I'll go out to the car and be ready to leave." I got up and thanked the host for a very nice meal and went upstairs to the exit door. I opened the door and held it open for one of the other guests, the minister Kenneth Baker, who was also leaving and just said, "After you, sir." As we went out of the restaurant, Kenneth Baker turned left and I turned right.

I walked about 15 yards to where my car was parked. As I was taking the keys from my pocket, I heard someone shouting. I turned to see who it was and saw four young men running across the Bayswater Road towards me. As they got closer, one shouted, "What did you call my mate?" I looked around to see who he was talking to, as I didn't think he was talking to me because I hadn't spoken. Then, as they surrounded me, one of the group suddenly came up to me and grabbed hold of my jacket lapels saying, "Give us your money."

Two of the other assailants were now kicking my legs to try to get me down on the ground. But the one that concerned me most of all was standing behind me with his right arm round my neck and I could also feel cold metal and something sharp cutting into my neck. As he was about the same height as me, his head was right up against my head and I could feel he had quite a lot of hair. So, with my right hand I grabbed his hair and quickly bent forward. He came over my head, and I heard him hit the pavement headfirst with a thud. Since the knife he was using was quite sharp, I didn't realise that he had cut my neck. In those days, I always wore a clip-on tie and the attacker in front of me had grabbed the tie which came off in his hand. I still didn't realise that the knife had cut my neck and by this time I was bleeding profusely. However, the man who was holding the tie saw all the blood And said, "I'm out of here." (Or words to that effect). They picked up their friend who had hit the ground and ran off down the side street dragging him as they went.

I bent down and picked up my tie and put it back on but didn't realise how badly my neck had been cut. I turned and walked back to the restaurant to let the police know what had happened. As I walked down the stairs in the restaurant, a lady let out a scream when she saw me as I was wearing a white shirt, which was now covered in blood. The restaurant manageress helped me downstairs to where Sir Geoffrey and his party were waiting. They all gathered around me very concerned. Somebody gave me a napkin to stem the blood and another guest held an ice pack to my neck. After hearing what had happened, the police officers rushed outside but the attackers had long gone. It was decided that I needed to go to hospital and just as we exited the restaurant the police car that had been on patrol came around the corner. I was quickly ushered into the car and taken to the local hospital, where I had to have nine stitches in the wound. I was told by the doctor that I was lucky as the knife must have had a small blade as the cut was long but not deep. To my surprise that night, I made the late-night news, where it was announced that Sir Geoffrey's driver had been attacked. I was later taken home from the hospital by the police.

The following day I went into work to pick up my car, as usual, but was told by the Superintendent to go home as I was not a pretty sight! Needless to say, Sir Geoffrey and Lady Howe were very concerned and rang me regularly at home to see how I was getting on. But other than a scar, which I still have today, I was none the worse for wear.

Fortunately, not all my experiences at that time were so dramatic. One morning as I was driving Sir Geoffrey into the office, he told me that he had been invited by Richard Attenborough to a preview showing off his new film 'Cry Freedom'. I think it was about a week later when we drove down to Richard Attenborough's House in Richmond. As we alighted from the car Sir Geoffrey asked if it would be all right if his driver could join them. Richard Attenborough gave a big smile and said, "Of course, there's plenty of room." After a chat and refreshments, he asked us to follow him and we walked out of the rear of his house and up a lighted pathway towards a building, which was his private cinema. We entered quite a large room and we all sat down in very comfortable armchairs. Our host gave a description of the film we were about to see, the lights dimmed and we proceeded to watch a most enjoyable film.

During my time with the Government Car Service, I had worked many times with the Special Branch, even in the "pool' when I was standing in for drivers who were sick or on leave. I became good friends with many of them over the years and still keep in touch with some of them even now. Many of the officers rose in rank. Some of them, who had been Sergeants when they worked with me, went on to become Superintendents or Chief Superintendents.

There was one occasion when I was driving Sir Geoffrey as Foreign Secretary, that there was a replacement Sergeant who came onto the team. He was very 'stroppy' and for some reason made it very plain that he did not like the Government Car Service drivers and quite often he would go the whole of his shift (Special Branch did two shifts, 07.00 until 14.00 and then a relief man would take over until the end of the day), and did not speak one word to me or any other GCS driver. It had always been arranged that when the Foreign Secretary had his meal, if in the city, embassy or hotel, that a Special Branch man would go ahead and organise a meal for himself and the driver. The reason for this was that the driver had to be on the spot at all times, wherever the Minister happened to be, so that if there was an emergency, we could be in the car and off immediately.

On the second occasion while working with this unfriendly officer, when I did not get a meal, I had a word with the Foreign Secretary's Private Secretary (I didn't bother the Foreign Secretary as he had enough on his plate), excuse the pun! He was very concerned and said he would have a word with the Sergeant explaining to him that the driver would usually start at seven o'clock every morning and work through to late at night and it was essential that he got his meals. This seemed to aggravate the Sergeant even more and he started to be very rude and offensive to all the GCS drivers. The crunch came for him one day when Sir Geoffrey had to leave the Foreign Office in a hurry and go to some buildings, which were on the other side of Whitehall (it used to be the old Scotland Yard buildings), to make an urgent news announcement from the studio there.

The normal procedure was that the Foreign Secretary's private office would press a button, which would ring a bell in the driver's room. The driver would immediately go out to the car and be ready to leave as the Minister came out of the door. The Private Secretary would also ring the protection officer to tell him that the Foreign Secretary was on the point of leaving. The protection officer's room was next to the Foreign Secretary's office and usually he would arrive at the car with the Foreign Secretary. But on this occasion, as the protection officer was obviously on the telephone, he could not be contacted. So when Sir Geoffrey came running out on his own and jumped into my car saying, "Okay, let's go, I need to get to the Norman Shaw buildings as quickly as you can," I immediately pointed out to him that the protection officer had not yet arrived. Sir Geoffrey just said. "Forget him, lets go," which I did.

When we arrived at the Norman Shaw building, Sir Geoffrey jumped out of the car and ran inside. I went straight over to the front door and asked the officer on duty if I could use the telephone as it was an emergency and he immediately agreed. I telephoned the Special Branch office in the Foreign Office but it was engaged. So I telephoned the driver's room at the Foreign Office and Lady Young's driver, who was a lady driver, answered. I said. "Would you do me a favour and run upstairs and tell Sir Geoffrey's protection officer that the Foreign Secretary is now in the Norman Shaw building, and he needs to get over here as soon as possible." I explained that I had already tried to ring him but the telephone was engaged. She said she would and ran up to the next floor and into the Special Branch office. Sir Geoffrey's protection officer was sitting in his chair with his feet up and was chatting on the telephone. Before the lady driver could speak, he shouted at her, "Get out, get out, you can see I'm on the phone!" Then after calling her a few choice words, he said." All you GCS drivers are the same, you don't know how to behave," followed by a few words which I cannot repeat. She was very upset by his remarks but said, "I've just come to tell you that the Foreign Secretary is at the Norman Shaw building and you need to get over there as soon as possible."

By this time I had turned my car around and was looking straight down the road towards The Foreign Office. Suddenly I noticed in the distance someone running at full pelt towards me. It was the officer in question, who managed to reach the car at the same time as Sir Geoffrey came out of the building and stepped briskly into the car saying, "I'll go back to the Foreign Office now, Peter."

This was not the end of the story because the lady driver, who drove Lady Young at the Foreign Office, was very angry and demanded an apology from the police officer. It was no surprise to discover soon afterwards that the Special Branch man had moved on to new pastures and I was certainly glad to see the back of him. A new officer soon arrived and life started to get back to normal.

When driving Sir Geoffrey, both as Chancellor and Foreign Secretary, I used to have to take him quite often on visits into the city of London for meetings, lunches and dinners. To start with, the journeys were quite straightforward, as after leaving Whitehall we could be in the city in about 15 to 20 minutes. However, once the IRA started letting off bombs, the timing of our arrival became very difficult as the police often introduced roadblocks and even redirections overnight. I remember once, after being caught out and arriving slightly late for one of Sir Geoffrey's appointments, it was agreed by Sir Geoffrey's protection team that there would be a different system for the next appointment. So after dropping of Sir Geoffrey in Downing Street for the night, we did a 'recce' and drove straight to the next day's drop-off point in the city. The protection officer wrote down the route and noted any changes that had been made from the usual way. Thus fully prepared, we made our way home for the night. The next day we set off confidently for the Foreign Office and as Sir Geoffrey came out to be taken for his city lunch, the protection officer said, "It's alright Sir, we won't be late today as we drove the route and checked it out last night." So off we drove. Unfortunately, as soon as we entered the City, we found our intended road was blocked off. Unbeknown to us, the city police had decided to close the road overnight. Fortunately, Sir Geoffrey was very understanding and thanked us for trying our best.

As I have said previously, I was very lucky on the whole with the Special Branch Officers I have worked with. However, some of the stories I've heard from them are hard to believe. In fact, if you put some of them into a film, people would say they are too far-fetched.

One particular protection officer, a Superintendent who accompanied Sir Geoffrey to a meeting overseas in a very high risk area, had a very interesting story to tell. He explained to me how when they arrived everyone in the party had been accommodated in a large gated house. In the evening, after everyone had gone to their rooms, the house was locked down and armed guards with dogs patrolled around the house all night. The officer told me that as it was a very hot night and he couldn't sleep, he opened his window, which was a long, door type and stepped out onto the ledge on the second floor in only his underpants, in order to try and cool off in the slight breeze. But to his horror, the breeze caught the window and slammed it shut.

Just then he heard voices from below, getting closer and closer and realised it was one of the ground patrols going around the building. He pressed himself back against the wall and hoped they would not look up and see a near naked man standing on an 18 inch ledge with all the windows shut! Fortunately, they continued around the corner of the building and didn't see him. He tried to get back into his room, but couldn't get the window open. He then decided to inch his way along the ledge to the next room. The window into this room was also shut, but he decided to tap on it in order to attract the guest. Luckily it was a man who recognised him and opened the window. The next day, everyone had a good laugh about the incident but it was pointed out that if he had gone to the right instead of the left on the ledge, the room was occupied by a lady and it might have taken some explaining from a man in his underpants, standing on an 18ins wide ledge and asking to be let in!

The same officer, let's call him John, went with Sir Geoffrey to India for an important funeral. It was an extremely hot day and while they were all standing in the shade of the canopy adjacent to the tent, the party were offered drinks. The Special Branch officer had been warned not to take any drinks unless, on taking off the cap of the bottle, there was a fizz of gas and bubbles (usually Schweppes tonic water).

John asked Sir Geoffrey, if he wanted a drink, and he replied, "Yes please". John turned to the man who was serving the drinks and said, "Two tonics, please." The man duly took a bottle opener and removed the cap. John took the drink and handed it to Sir Geoffrey. He then returned to the man, who proceeded to hand him the second bottle, but this one already had the cap off. It was only later that John noticed the same man filling other bottles from a goatskin! Unfortunately, when Sir Geoffrey arrived back at Heathrow, John came off the plane on a stretcher and was very poorly for quite a long time.

I must say that during my time with Sir Geoffrey, from the time he became Foreign Secretary until my retirement, there was never a dull moment or a fixed routine. For example, sometimes when Sir Geoffrey was due to attend a meeting, he would travel there by aeroplane. On these occasions his Private Office would call me to explain that as Sir Geoffrey would be returning home by light aircraft, he would like me to meet him at one of the small airfields situated close to London. I remember on one occasion, I was asked to pick him up at an airfield close to the M40 near High Wycombe quite late in the evening.

So I got the map out, jumped in the car and off I went. I was well aware that the main trouble with going to a small airfield at night time was trying to find your way in. Nevertheless, on this occasion that proved to be no problem. But once inside, I started to get a bit concerned as there were no lights on and the whole place looked deserted. I think the plane was due to land at about 10.30 p.m., but when it got to that time, there was still no sign of any lights and the place remained deserted. I started to think that I'd got the wrong airfield, so I got out of the car wondering what I should do next. Suddenly, to my amazement, all the lights came on, including the runway lights. Almost immediately I spotted a plane approaching, which landed and taxied up close to where I was standing. The door opened and Sir Geoffrey stepped out, followed by the pilot. I just said. "Thank goodness, I thought I had the wrong place as everything looked deserted." The pilot said, "It is." When I asked who had put the lights on, he replied, "I did - by remote control from the aircraft." At least that was another panic over.

Whilst I was allocated to Sir Geoffrey, at the Foreign Office, there was another very memorable occasion that started when he was picked up one day by a helicopter in London and then taken, I believe, to a destination somewhere in the north of England. On his return journey, the helicopter was due to land him at an airfield, where I would meet him and then take him on to his home in Warwickshire. The Foreign Office gave me a map and also the address of the airfield, which they told me was an RAF airfield.

So I got my things together, had a good look at the map I had been given and made a note of the route I would take. I set off as soon as possible, since it was quite a long way to go and it was also the time of the year when it got dark at about seven o'clock. Luckily I had a good journey and eventually arrived at the nearest village on the map to the airfield. But try as I might, I couldn't find the airfield. I was getting a bit concerned by now and began to think I had got the wrong place (there were no mobile phones then).

Suddenly I noticed a man coming out of a farm gate with his dog. I stopped the car, got out and went over there to him and said, "Good evening sir. I wonder if you can help me. I'm looking for the RAF airfield." He looked back at me with a big smile on his face and said, "You're a bit late lad. There was an RAF airfield here, but it shut down about 15 years ago." I explained to him that I was supposed to meet somebody there. He said. "Well, the old buildings are still there." He continued that if I went down the road for about 200 yards, I would see a track on the left hand side. He told me to go down that and I would reach what was left of the old buildings. I thanked him and followed his directions down to the buildings he had described, but the place was completely deserted.

By now, it was just starting to get dark and I was getting quite worried. Then I noticed, about half a mile away, a helicopter circling around with what looked like a bright light shining down from it. I immediately jumped into my car and drove it up an old ramp I'd noticed nearby, so that my headlights were now facing up at the helicopter. I then started flashing my lights, high beam on and off. To my great relief, the helicopter pilot turned his beam to face my direction and started flashing back. Within a few minutes, the helicopter had landed quite close by in an open space and Sir Geoffrey and the pilot stepped out. The pilot said, "That was a close thing. We were just about to give up!"

When I got back to London, I went into the private office and had a moan saying, "I think you need to update your maps as it was just sheer luck that I found the old airfield." However, I think that by then Sir Geoffrey had already had a word with them!

As Sir Geoffrey's permanent allocated driver, I was discovering that there was no such thing as a daily routine. For example, I remember one time when Sir Geoffrey was going to Brussels for a meeting. He sometimes used an RAF aircraft from RAF Northolt airfield. I would drive his party of officials to the airport, where he would fly out, have a meeting over lunch, then return. Sometimes, it wasn't worth my while driving back to London because by the time I got to Whitehall, I would have to turn around and drive back to Northolt. On this particular occasion Sir Geoffrey said to me as we were approaching Northolt by car, "What do you do when we go to Brussels?" I replied that I would just park up, get a newspaper, have a cup of tea and wait until he returned. He then said, "Well this time, why don't you park the car and come with us and you can join us for lunch in Brussels?" I jumped at the offer because it was a long time since I had been in an RAF aircraft. So off we went.

Sir Geoffrey had his meeting and I had tea and lunch with his protection officer. Once the meeting was over, we returned to our RAF plane, which immediately took off. As we were crossing over the Channel, the pilot said that the weather was closing in very quickly and it had started to snow. Nothing much more was said until we were approaching Northolt airfield, when I heard the dreaded words, "We might not be able to land because of the snow." This would have been very inconvenient as our armoured car was parked next to the guard room. The private secretary went up to the pilot and said, "If you could land at Northolt, it would be much appreciated." The pilot said, "Okay, I'll give it a go", which he did and fortunately made a perfect landing. So ended yet another unexpectedly interesting day for me. By now I was really enjoying the excitement and the lack of routine in my job. No day could be boring, as I never knew what might be happening next.

In 1989, the Russian President, Mikhail Gorbachev and his wife, Raisa, visited this country and Sir Geoffrey had talks with him. Raisa was known to be very interested in British history so it was decided to give them both lunch at Hampton Court.

After the meal and while Sir Geoffrey was having talks with President Gorbachev, it had been arranged to give Raisa a full tour of the Palace. So we were soon met by one of the senior guides to show us around. Lady Howe turned to me and said "I'm sure you would like to join us Peter as I know you're very interested in history." I answered, "Thank you very much. I'd be absolutely delighted." I was then introduced to Mrs Gorbachev, who I found to be an absolutely charming person. She took a great interest in all aspects of the tour and asked many relevant questions about the building and people who had lived there. After the tour had ended, we met up again with Sir Geoffrey and Mr Gorbachev and had tea together before leaving. Later, I thanked Sir Geoffrey for a very memorable day and said I had been very privileged to have been invited to join them. Of course this generous action was not unusual because Sir Geoffrey always made sure that I was well looked after and tried to include me whenever possible.

On another occasion, Sir Geoffrey told me that he had been invited to the Royal Ascot race meeting. This was good news for the protection officer and me as we had never been there before. The big day soon arrived and we set off for the Ascot meeting. It was a beautiful sunny day as we drove in and parked in the secure area for VIP cars. Sir Geoffrey and Lady Howe got out of the car and went up to the VIP balcony and found the suite number indicated on the invitation. Sir Geoffrey turned to us and said, "I'm sure there will be room for you to join us." However, when the hostess opened the door, we found that the room was completely packed with people. Sir Geoffrey turned to us and said, "Oh, sorry. There doesn't seem to be room for you after all," as he and Lady Howe went inside and the hostess shut the door.

We stood outside deciding what to do next, as the rule was we had to be close to Sir Geoffrey in case of any emergency. Just then we noticed a young lady coming towards us. As she approached, she said, "Can I help you?" The protection officer said who we were and explained that the VIP suite was full. She thought for a moment and then said, "Okay, just wait there a few minutes."

A short time later she returned and said, "Apparently the suite next door isn't being used," as she led us over, opened the door and took us inside. "I will arrange for some lunch to be brought over to you," she said. We thanked her and opened the door onto the balcony where there was a table and chairs set out. We were delighted to find that we were overlooking the racetrack, very close to the finishing post. The hostess then said, "I'll see you later," pointed to a coffee machine and continued, "Help yourself." We settled down to drink our coffee and soon afterwards there was a knock on the door. I opened it and a lady pushed in a trolley saying, "This is your lunch, gentlemen."

We couldn't believe our luck and happily carried our food outside onto the table on the balcony. We had just about finished our lunch, with our array of empty plates still spread out on the table, when we heard the door opening on the adjoining balcony of the suite next door. A crowd of extremely smartly dressed ladies and gentlemen, streamed out onto the balcony until it was absolutely packed. I noticed St Geoffrey and Lady Howe amongst the crowd. He looked over at us in amazement and I just waved back.

Once the race meeting was over and Sir Geoffrey was about to leave, we went outside and waited until he came out of his suite. When he saw us, he smiled and said, "How did you manage to pull that off and get the suite next door to us all to yourselves?" We explained what had happened and he said, "Well done. I'm glad you managed to get your lunch." We thanked him for our excellent day out, which must have been a lot more comfortable than for the VIP guests!

18 SIR GEOFFREY HOWE'S DISMISSAL FROM THE FOREIGN OFFICE

On Monday morning, 24 July 1989, I picked up Sir Geoffrey as usual, between 7.30 and 8.00 a.m. at his residence and took him to the Foreign Office building in Whitehall and duly parked the car in our designated space in the Foreign Office courtyard. I got out of the car and walked up to the first floor with Sir Geoffrey, as my room was just a few doors from his office and this gave me a chance to discuss our movements for the day or week ahead. As we neared his office, I said, "I have heard the Prime Minister is to have a reshuffle this week." He turned to me as he was about to open his door and said, "Yes, but I don't think it affects me" and he disappeared inside his office.

I continued along the corridor for about 50 yards to the driver's room, immediately putting the kettle on to make a cup of tea. The door to the corridor was still open as I waited for the kettle to boil. Suddenly I heard footsteps on the marble floor coming in my direction. The driver's room was the last room along the corridor and next to the staircase that lead down to Downing Street. I put my head round the door just as Sir Geoffrey came level with me. I said, "Are you going out, sir" and he replied, "It's okay. I'm just going over to No. 10." My heart sank and I thought to myself, "I don't like the look of this."

I went back into my room and turned the kettle off and then returned to the top of the stairs. I don't know how long I stood there, but it seemed like an eternity. Eventually, I heard footsteps coming back up the staircase and Sir Geoffrey walked towards me. He said, "Come with me." We went to his office and walked in and he said, "Shut the door", which I did. He looked at me and said, "I am no longer the Foreign Secretary."

For a few seconds, I just stood there not knowing what to say. Then I said, "So, what job have you got?" He said, "Leader of the House." I then said the words, "But that's not a job!" I know I shouldn't have said this, but I was very upset as I thought he deserved better. I was later told that Sir Geoffrey would also be Deputy Prime Minister and Lord President of the Privy Council.

After losing his position as Foreign Secretary, Sir Geoffrey retained his police protection and official car, as he was still high on the I.R.A. hit list and we were on full alert at all times. However, he did have to vacate his official residence at Carlton Gardens. So the next problem for him and Lady Howe was to find somewhere else to live that was fairly close to the House of Commons. This was not an easy task as they would still have to continue with police protection outside his house when he was in residence and the house itself needed to have a lot of security work done, including a safe room.

Unfortunately, it was probably inevitable that there would be some low points as well as many highs in the job. Amongst Sir Geoffrey and Lady Howe's closest friends were Jane and Ian Gow, who was the MP for Eastbourne. Ian Gow was a lovely man and I'd been to his house, 'The Dog House' near Eastbourne, on a few occasions and he and Jane Gow always made the police and myself most welcome. My only grumble with him was when the House of Commons had risen late at night, he would often pass by me as he walked through to Sir Geoffrey's room, and I would call this the 'Gow factor', which meant that I knew I would be there for at least another hour, while they discussed the latest political situation with regard to Europe. Sir Geoffrey later used my expression in his memoirs when he wrote:

"In my room in the House, after the Commons had risen, we would often linger over a glass of whisky, trying to make sense of our common dilemma. The 'Gow factor'- which kept me so often late at night and which Peter Smithson, my long-suffering driver knew so well - became ever more evident in my year as Leader of the House."

On Monday 30th July 1990 as the House of Commons was in recess and Sir Geoffrey Howe was at home, I took a few days leave. Early in the morning, the telephone rang and it was Sir Geoffrey to inform me sadly that his great friend, Ian Gow, had been blown up. We were to later find out that it was an action by the IRA.

I asked, "Is he dead?" and he replied, "Yes, I believe so." I said, "I'll come and pick you up as soon as possible. I assume you want to go there straight away." "Yes", he said quietly. I drove straight to his home where his protection officers were waiting and we left for Eastbourne.

Our journey down there passed mostly in thoughtful silence, both still shocked at the dreadful news. When we arrived at the 'Dog House', his Eastbourne home, the place was crawling with police and firemen, who were examining the damage and clearing the site. I got talking to one of the police officers and he told me that Mrs Gow had been telling him that they owned two cars and that Ian had telephoned the local garage on the Friday to ask them to come and pick up one of the cars for servicing. Fortunately for the mechanic who came to pick up the car, he took the wrong one. If he had taken the car he was supposed to, it would have been him that was blown up, rather than Ian Gow.

Soon after this event, I was surprised to be told that Sir Geoffrey had lost his Special Branch protection. A short while later, I was taking him to a meeting in Whitehall when he said to me, "Peter, I've been told that I'm going to lose my government car in a few weeks time." I was quite shocked to hear this, as we were always being told to take care as the IRA had him on their hit list and they had already proved their intentions with Ian Gow. In fact, at a later date I was given a newspaper cutting with an article describing how the IRA had said that on one occasion they had been all set up and ready to assassinate Sir Geoffrey in his car. However, they said it did not take place because the driver was very late picking up Sir Geoffrey and it had to be called off. This was not true because I was never late picking up my boss. I should imagine the truth was that we very rarely kept to the same route or time and made many variations on our way to a destination, in order to make such an attack on him very difficult.

As Sir Geoffrey got out of the car and walked into the Cabinet office in Whitehall, I sat there trying to let the news sink in and wondering what to do. Just then somebody tapped on my car's side window and I looked up to see John Kerr, who used to be Sir Geoffrey's Private Secretary at the Foreign Office. I couldn't believe my luck as John, I thought, was now working for Prime Minister John Major at No. 10. I immediately got out of the car and said "I'm really glad to see you. They have just told the boss that somebody has made the decision to remove his protection car." John listened, looking quite surprised and said, "Don't go away, I'll be back," and he went straight back into the Cabinet office. About 15 minutes later he returned and came up to me and said, "I've had a word, and Geoffrey can keep his protection car." I was pleasantly surprised and thanked him as he continued, "I'm in a bit of a rush but give Geoffrey my best regards." Later John Kerr became our ambassador in Washington, U.S.A. and was eventually elevated to the House of Lords.

About half an hour later, Sir Geoffrey came out of his meeting and got into my car. I started the engine but before driving off I turned round and said, "By the way Sir. You will be keeping your car for the foreseeable future." He looked at me with some surprise and said, "How do you know?" I continued telling him how just after he went into the meeting, John Kerr had appeared and when I told him about the car, he had seemed very cross and went straight back into the office." I continued with some relish explaining that a short time later he had come back out and said, "Tell Sir Geoffrey, he is keeping his car." We were both in a contented mood as we drove off and I'm certainly glad to say that he kept his car for quite a long time after that incident.

I was very annoyed to read several newspaper reports over the years that followed, which tried to make out that Sir Geoffrey himself had actively taken steps to keep his car. Or, as one well known daily newspaper stated after Howe had been elevated to the House of Lords,

"I suspect Lord Howe still has a limo because the self-important booby wanted one and was prepared to make enough fuss".

To my knowledge, he never made any fuss, or indeed any attempts whatsoever to keep his car and, as several security papers were later to confirm, his government car had to be continued for several years because of the prolonged security risk. The sad assassinations of Ian Gow and Airey Neave would only confirm the truth of the risk assessments.

19 THE HOUSE OF LORDS

Eventually in 1992, when Sir Geoffrey decided to retire from the House of Commons, he was elevated to the House of Lords where he took the title of Baron Howe of Aberavon. Soon afterwards, he told me that we had to go to the College of Arms in Queen Victoria Street in order to discuss the design of his coat of arms. After parking in the courtyard, we walked over towards the historic building and the now Lord Howe invited me to come in with him to have a look around as he thought I would find it very interesting. Once his meeting had finished, we returned to his office. Later he showed me his completed coat of arms, which included a wolf's head covered by a sheep's fleece (a wolf in sheep's clothing!) I was amazed and amused to see how he had exacted revenge on his old friend but political rival, Denis Healey, who had famously quoted that to be attacked by Sir Geoffrey Howe in parliamentary speeches was, "Like being savaged by a dead sheep." No doubt Margaret Thatcher might also reflect ruefully that his coat of arms was a somewhat more accurate description of his character than the flippant quote!

This reminds me of one of the interesting coincidences that Lord Howe recounted to me after his return from a holiday in Venice. After a long day visiting many of the sights in the town, he arrived in St. Mark's Square. Situated at one end, there is a large column with seats around the base. He decided to sit down there and take in the amazing view of the square. After a few moments, he thought he heard a familiar voice speaking in English and looked over his shoulder, only to see Denis Healey sitting behind him! They couldn't believe the coincidence of two former Chancellors of the Exchequer sitting down on the same bench at the same time in Venice, without either knowing the other was even visiting the country.

Another interesting coincidence occurred at this time when I was taking Lord Howe to his office in Berkley Square. He told me he had been invited to lunch the next day by one of his former colleagues at the Foreign Office and gave me a piece of paper with the address written on it. I could not believe my eyes as it was exactly the same address, 66, Richbourne Terrace, where I had lived with my parents as a child! However, we occupied only the basement and three more families lived on the three floors above.

When we arrived, Lord Howe explained to his host that I had used to live there and he immediately invited me to join them inside. Very kindly he showed us around and I could hardly believe my eyes at the changes that had been made! We went downstairs to the basement to see what used to be our bedroom, sitting room and small kitchen was now one large kitchen-diner. The whole house was absolutely beautiful. I reflected ruefully how before we were re-housed to a three bedroom flat in a council block near Vauxhall, my father had been offered this house in Richbourne Terrace for £1,250 and now it must be worth over one million pounds!

There continued to be never a dull moment whilst driving Lord and Lady Howe. It was always a case of expect the unexpected. I remember one Friday night in November and the day of my 60th birthday. As usual, I would take him to his home in Warwickshire. Normally we would leave in the late afternoon to get him there by about six o'clock. As we got into the car in Downing Street, Lord Howe said that he needed to call in at Carlton Gardens to see somebody. So off we went and as we pulled up at the front door, a police officer opened the door and Lord Howe, together with Lady Howe, alighted and went inside the building. I thought it was rather strange as the place looked deserted except for the police officer on duty inside.

Expecting to leave quite soon, I sat patiently in the car but after about 15 minutes I decided to go inside to see what was happening. I spoke to the police officer and asked who else was there but he seemed a bit 'offish'. Just then, the hall telephone rang and the policemen answered it. He then turned to me and said, "It's for you." I answered the 'phone and it was Lord Howe. He asked me to get his official Red Box out of the car and bring it upstairs to the first floor. I said that I would and turned to the police officer saying, "We're going to be here all night, at this rate."

I collected the box from the car and ran up the long staircase to the first floor. As I opened the door, to my amazement, the very large room was absolutely packed with people and to the sound of bagpipes, they all sang 'Happy Birthday'. There must have been 150 people in there, including all my family and friends and, I believe, most of the government ministers that I had driven over the years. Lord Howe then made a very complimentary speech about me which I will never forget. Then they called for me to say a few words. I tried, but I must say I was absolutely overcome with emotion. Lord Howe explained that he had also organised a relief driver to take him on to his home in Warwickshire, so that I was able to have a drink and enjoy myself

I tried to get round the room to meet everybody, but there were so many people there it would have taken me all night, so I just had to do my best. I was amazed that Lord Howe had managed to arrange it so that there were no cars about or any evidence that there was somebody in the building. In addition, both he and my wife must have spent a lot of time organising the party. But that was just typical of the Howes. They were always very thoughtful and generous to their friends and staff. I never heard them say a bad word about anyone. In fact, I always felt whilst working for Lord Howe that he was not just my boss but also my good friend.

On Monday, 11 May 1998, I was driving my car to Chesham Place as I had an invitation to a party that Lady Thatcher was giving for her driver and my good friend, Denis Oliver, to mark his retirement after 42 years service in the Government Car Service. Denis remembered that I had helped Lady Thatcher out when she was a PPS at the Ministry of Pensions by giving her a push start in her private car several times before finally deciding to fit a new battery for her, which solved the problem for both of us! Just as I was approaching the venue, I saw Denis and gave him a toot on the horn. He came over to me and said, "I'm glad you were able to come." We parked my car and Denis asked the policeman on the door to keep an eye on it.

We went inside, number 36 Chesham Place, which was quite full of people and went through to the main reception room. As we entered, Denis said, "Oh, there's Mrs. Thatcher by the window." We walked up to her just as she was finishing talking to a gentleman. She turned to Denis and he introduced me saying, "This is my friend of many years, Peter Smithson. You've probably forgotten as it must be 30 years ago, but he helped you with your car when you were at the Ministry of Pensions." She said, "Oh hello and who do you drive now?" I replied, "Geoffrey Howe." The smile immediately left her face and she turned and walked to the other side of the room. I was very surprised as any disagreements she might have with my boss had nothing to do with me. Denis looked at me and said, "Sorry about that." But I just shrugged my shoulders, had a cup of coffee and walked out to my car.

I was now well past normal retirement age but still enjoying my job and reluctant for my very exciting and interesting way of life to come to an end. In addition, Lord Howe seemed keen that I should continue to be his driver. Thus far, I had managed to avoid the thorny question of retirement. However, one day I went along to the Government Car Service headquarters in Vauxhall as my car needed a service. Lord Howe was in a meeting all day, so I told the workshop that I would go and have lunch in the canteen while they worked on the car. As I walked in, the GCS Superintendent and his Deputy saw me and called me over. They invited me to join them and the conversation soon got around to my length of service and when I intended to retire as I was now past 65 years of age. I replied, "I've been thinking about that lately but I do enjoy my job. So how about on my 70th Birthday?" This seemed to satisfy them and the Superintendent said that was alright, provided I passed my medical each year, which I did. However, inevitably the day of my 70th Birthday eventually arrived and I kept to my word with a reluctant retirement.

Lord Howe told me that he and Lady Howe would like to organise a farewell party for me at The House of Lords, together with family, friends and colleagues, including some of the past Ministers I had worked for. I thanked him for his kindness and said that would be absolutely marvellous. When the day arrived, we had a most memorable occasion and once again Lord Howe made a very flattering speech about my career in front of the large gathering of guests. I had also prepared a speech to thank numerous people I had worked with over the years but the atmosphere was so emotional that I had to cut it short. However, I did say how lucky I had been to work for Lord Howe for 24 years, without us ever having a cross word, and that I always felt I had been treated like one of the family.

THE ORDERS OF KNIGHTHOOD
ST JAMES'S PALACE, S.W.1.

14th October, 2003

Sir,

I am commanded to forward the Imperial Service Medal which Her Majesty The Queen has been graciously pleased to award to you in recognition of the meritorious services which you have rendered.

I have the honour to be, Sir, Your obedient servant,

Robert Cartwright

Registrar of the Imperial Service Order.

Peter John William Smithson, Esq., BEM

Notification of the Imperial Service Medal

With Angela at Goodwood Revival Show, 2011

**With new French owner of my XK120 & Angela,
on Pyrenees Rally, 2010**

With Mike Marshall Ride in chateau near Cannes, 2010

Outside Caroline & Quentin's Chateau in Normandy, 2010

With Angela & Denis Oliver at GCS Reunion, 2011

Joy Lofthouse, Angela, Howard Bush at Bomber Command Memorial Unveiling, London 2012

20 RETIREMENT

Retiring after 43 years of service and at the age of 70 was quite an upheaval after being used to having my day ordered from seven o'clock in the morning until midnight or sometimes even later. In addition, my holidays had been very few and far between and I very rarely had weekends off. Such unsocial hours and lengthy stays away from home had, over a period of time, almost inevitably led to an estrangement between myself and my wife Maureen, which led first to our separation and then our divorce.

Although I had been able to pursue several hobbies during my career, in particular my interest in restoring classic cars and oil painting, my other keen interests, for example in history, (particularly military history), the RAF and travel had usually been restricted to reading books rather than something more proactive. My retirement now gave me a chance for this to change and to enjoy participating more actively in these interests.

I was a member of the RAF 7 Squadron Association and could now for the first time join in most of their events. This had the happy consequence of not only allowing me to renew acquaintance with some of my old comrades from my service at RAF Tengah in Singapore, Malaya, and to make new friends, but also to meet my second wife, Angela, who was also a member of the Association. Her Uncle had been a navigator in Bomber Command during the Second World War and membership of this club was one of the many varied hobbies she followed. We were delighted to discover that we had many additional interests in common and over time we realised that we were destined to spend the rest of our lives together. Eventually in 2009 we got married in the lovely Staffordshire town of Lichfield, in an area where Angela had lived and worked as a teacher for most of her life.

Like many things in life, my membership of the RAF 7 Squadron Association had come about through pure luck rather than intention. Having read various articles in the newspapers about the lack of equipment our troops were suffering when involved in wars abroad, I wrote a letter to the Daily Mail telling of the similar situation I had faced many years earlier in Singapore, Malaya, when I had been told I had to do guard duty that night at a 'bomb dump', which had been attacked the previous day by terrorists. With only two Malayan soldiers to help me, I had been issued with just 5 rounds of ammunition, as apparently we could not risk ammunition falling into the hands of the enemy.

Following the publication of my letter, I received many letters back from people who had read this in the newspaper. A couple seemed keen to point out that RAF Tengah was in Singapore, not Malaya. However, as my posting was to Malaya, the stamps to post letters home said Malaya, and I was eventually issued with a GSM medal with a bar stating Malaya on it, I assumed that Singapore was at that time part of Malaya. Amongst other correspondence was a letter from Ron Mole, the Secretary of the RAF 7 Squadron Association, who coincidentally had served with me at RAF Tengah at the same time, encouraging me to join the group. I agreed to do so and was quickly reunited with several of the airman I had served with in Malaya. This included one gentleman, Mike Marshall-Ride, a real character who had been a pilot out there and later became a Squadron Leader. Despite his advancing years and the fact that he now lives in Majorca, he still manages to turn up at many of our events.

Although 7 Squadron had been a bomber squadron during World War 2, the need for such planes had gradually diminished and the Squadron is now involved in flying Chinook helicopters, based in Odiham. The Association is proud of its close links with the present brave pilots and airman, who have been involved with distinction in so many of the recent wars and has been keen to develop this important relationship. Thus it is that I have been able to enjoy several visits to the base with my wife and other members of the Association in order to enjoy their hospitality and, on special occasions, to witness their skills at first hand during the air shows held there.

We are also proud to join the Association as often as possible when they march at the Cenotaph on Remembrance Day each year. Even aged former airmen from as far away as Canada manage to join us and we usually continue to renew acquaintances afterwards at a local hostelry!

A trip to the 'Bomber Command Memorial and Unveiling' in Green Park, London, in June 2012 also gave us an opportunity to meet up with other friends from our Association, who had been invited. One lady, Joy Lofthouse, was a member of the Air Transport Auxiliary (A.T.A.) and ferried spitfires and numerous other fighters and bombers between bases during the Second World War. She has many interesting tales to recount. Apparently it was quite common to be asked to pilot an aircraft type she had never flown before. She once climbed into a bomber and had only the handbook balanced on her knee to tell her the relevant essential information required to fly and land the machine. Quite often when she alighted at her destination, she would be greeted with astonishment by the ground crew, whose first words would be, "But you're a woman!", when she took off her flying helmet. She married a very well respected and popular commanding officer of 7 Squadron,

Charles Lofthouse, and so keeps her close links with the Association to this day. Although now in her 90's she is still extremely active and has featured in several recent television documentaries about Bomber Command. Another friend of ours, Howard Bush, gave a television interview at the end of the televised programme covering the Memorial Unveiling as his father, who was a Lancaster navigator during the war, was sadly shot down, killed and buried in Berlin before Howard was born.

In addition to these activities, I have also been able to increase my life-long enjoyment of classic cars by actually having the time to join in the activities of several clubs – the Jaguar XK Club, the Jaguar Enthusiasts' Club and the Surrey Vintage Vehicle Club amongst others. This has not only served to enlarge my group of like-minded friends but has also enabled me to take part in several Classic Car tours and rallys in this country and abroad. The most successful of these events for me was probably the Classic Jaguar London to Brighton Run in 2008, when I was surprised and delighted to win in my beloved XK120, 'The Peoples' Choice Cup', for the car people would most like to take home with them.

However, my most exciting tour was probably the Strasbourg 'Entente Cordiale' event in 2010 in my restored 1952 Jaguar XK120 OTS (open top sport). This car really lives up to its name and I would suggest is much more of a sports car than modern day equivalents. The rush that you get from travelling at high speed along a country road with the canvas top down, the wind blowing in your hair and the noise from its 3 litre engine is quite something. Even more so when you are negotiating the sharp, hilly turns of an Ardennes forest road, with no power steering or power assisted brakes, with a heavy clutch, and whilst desperately trying to keep up with or indeed ahead of some modern Jaguars, with their very determined drivers. The experience results in quite an adrenaline rush. Fortunately, my hours of loving restoration and money lavished on the car over the years came into their own, not only with regard to its reliability but also with the confidence I could drive it on the edge in some difficult conditions.

However, the experience had served to teach me that driving an XK120 OTS was probably more for younger people and that the time had finally come for me to reluctantly say goodbye to it. So it came about, that after advertising the car for a short while in 2010, I had an enquiry from an extremely pleasant gentleman in France, called Michel, who was acting as the intermediary for the mayor in a southern French town near the Pyrenees.

I had prepared the car to such a high standard that when Michel and a friend arrived to examine it, he simply walked round the car, listened to the engine and immediately phoned up the mayor with his positive recommendation and was told to buy it. To my amazement, they informed me that they were going to drive it straight down to the south of France the next day. I knew the car was in excellent condition, but it had never been driven on such a long continuous journey before and I was very relieved when I heard that they arrived back home without any incident.

The mayor was so delighted with the car that when he heard that my wife and I were intending to do a four week tour of France that year, he invited us to join him with his local classic car club on a rally through the Pyrenees and also to spend a few days at the home of his friend, Michel, who I had already met and his family.

On the way down, we had been invited to stay with a couple of my friends, Lord Howe's former Private Secretary, Caroline and her husband Quentin, in their impressive chateau in Normandy. They have both worked tremendously hard to renovate and maintain this beautiful building to an exceptionally high standard and the grounds and buildings are open for part of each year to groups or individual guests to enjoy this magnificent hotel and its grounds. When we arrived we were extremely fortunate to find that we had the whole chateau to ourselves. Apparently Rommel had made it his headquarters during parts of the Second World War and you could well understand the reason why, as we stood at the windows of the magnificent main bedroom, looking out over the extensive grounds, watching the huge carp swimming around in the beautiful lake as the evening sunlight glinted off the surface.

After a delicious evening meal, complete with a generous amount of wine, during which we were able to catch up on news of their delightful family, I reminded Quentin of the time he had played his bagpipes as a musical greeting when I entered the room at my 60th birthday party at Carlton Gardens. Angela said she would very much like to hear him playing and no sooner the word than the deed. As we made our way up the magnificent spiral staircase to bed, Quentin regaled us with a selection of tunes on his bagpipes. An experience not to be forgotten!

The next day, Caroline and Quentin were off to visit one of their daughters, who was at university at Rome. However, they explained that we were welcome to stay on and that their son Rory was on vacation and would be coming to join us later that day. Handing us the keys to the chateau and with a brief instructions regarding the visit of the laundry lady, we waved them off and stood for a few moments surveying the now empty chateau and its grounds. We decided to make the most of the sunny day and sat outside relaxing, having lunch and wandering around the beautiful grounds.

Eventually, Rory turned up and what a delightful young man he turned out to be! Good looking, very intelligent and with a fantastic, good-humoured personality just like his parents. After several hours of very congenial conversation, discussing his university life, travels around the continent, and all manner of things, it was time for us to go up to our room to change ready for our evening meal. When we descended the staircase we could hear what we thought was a radio programme, with a beautiful piano solo being played. As we walked into the drawing room, to our great astonishment, there was Rory, seated at the piano and playing without any sheet music. Was there no end to his talents!

The next day we set off to travel for a few days down to the neighbourhood of Poitiers where Margaret, an old school friend of

Angela's, had set up home with her husband. They had been hard at work for some time restoring the old village bakery into their new home and it was delightful to be able to join them for a meal while catching up on all the news and then to stay overnight.

After breakfast we set off on and took a couple of days to drive down towards the Pyrenees to meet up with our friend Michel and his delightful family. In typical French style, we were introduced to various members of their family, who came specially to visit us and that evening we all sat outside to enjoy a typically sumptuous French meal. The next morning we were up bright and early to meet up with the rest of their local classic car club. We were pleasantly surprised to find that they had arranged for an English gentleman, Cedric Philp, who lived in the neighbourhood with his American wife, Barbara, to drive us on the tour in their classic Bentley. They proved to be a most interesting and well travelled couple with whom we have continued to keep in touch.

At our first stop, I spotted my beloved Jaguar XK 120 roadster parked up beside a variety of other classic cars. It looked beautiful and it was obvious that the mayor had taken a considerable amount of trouble to keep it in tiptop condition. I was told by somebody that the car even had a room of its own in his house, although I'm not quite sure whether that was true or not! A few minutes later we met up with the mayor himself, who proved to be a charming man and seemed delighted to meet us. Unfortunately, he hardly spoke any English, so it was left mainly to my wife, who used to be a French teacher, to do most of the chatting and to translate for us. It certainly seemed that what I had heard about French mayors was true, as he appeared to be a most powerful figure, to whom everybody gave the utmost respect.

After a most enjoyable drive through the beautiful countryside of the Pyrenees, we eventually drew up at the hotel where we were to spend the night. An informal reception with drinks and snacks was held outside in the sun drenched courtyard, during which the mayor and various club dignitaries made their speeches before we all made our way up the road to a local restaurant for another delicious meal.

The next morning, we continued our rally back through winding roads to the Hotel de Ville, where the mayor had laid on a room and facilities for the presentation of trophies. Angela and I were called out to the front of the hall, where the mayor made a gracious speech regarding his new-found English friends. We were then presented with various small gifts, several with the town's coat of arms, printed on them as obviously the mayor was doing his best to cement the Entente Cordiale! Afterwards, he invited the two of us into the mayor's parlour, where I handed over my gift to him of a small model of a Jaguar XK120 and an illustrated book about XKs, which seemed to please him very much. We had been made to feel like honoured guests, and I must say I was most impressed with everybody's friendliness and hospitality, which continued into the next day as we were invited to return to Michel's house to stay with them for another night. The following morning we were ready to set off again, only to be presented with several jars of 'foie gras' and bottles of excellent French wine just as we were about to drive away.

Continuing along the south coast of France and the Cote d'Azur, whilst stopping overnight at several pleasant locations, we eventually reached our next destination, where Mike Marshall-Ride, my friend from 7 Squadron Association, was staying with a friend in her chateau just inland from Cannes. From a distance it looked magnificent as it stood on top of a very steep hill with a commanding position over the lovely countryside beneath.

However, the roads which led up to it were extremely narrow and winding. In fact at one stage, I thought my normally excellent navigator, Angela, had taken us the wrong way up a one way road. This proved not to be the case when we joined a queue of traffic moving slowly uphill as a small lorry came down towards us, trying to negotiate one of the tight corners!

Eventually we arrived safely at the top, to be met by Mike, my former officer from RAF Tengah, Singapore. We were shown into a beautiful bedroom and told that we must have a meal with them and stay the night. It seemed very strange to have a Squadron Leader asking me, a former S.A.C., which daily newspaper I would like him to go and buy for me and then to be served breakfast by him the next morning on his lovely patio in such an idyllic situation! Although well into his 80s, Mike still looks and keeps very fit and enjoys playing tennis nearly every day. So it was no surprise when he gazed wistfully down towards the small airfield at the bottom of the hill and explained how he was thinking about buying himself a small plane to fly here from his base in Majorca!

Eventually the time came to leave and we enjoyed an uneventful, but most interesting journey, continuing through France into Italy and then back northwards into Switzerland and finally back home after a delightful four-week holiday.

I have always been interested in politics and my retirement, gave me the chance to become an active member of a couple of local Conservative clubs. In addition, I hear regularly from Lord and Lady Howe, and always try to visit them at home when we are in the Midlands. They kindly invite Angela and me to their Christmas parties and family occasions, never miss sending me a birthday or Christmas card, and have always been two of the most pleasant people you could wish to meet. In addition, Diana Holderness (the widow of my former well liked boss Richard Wood, later Lord Holderness) also keeps in touch and recently invited us to lunch in her lovely home in Windsor for a helpful chat as she is a Private Publisher. It is interesting how over the years I have nearly always found the Conservative ministers I worked for to be the most kind and considerate of bosses, treating me as an equal, even though many of them had an aristocratic or public school background. I think the only one outstanding exception was the Minister of Labour, John Hare. However, I must say I was also very lucky with the Labour ministers, who I was allocated to drive and were a pleasure to work for, such as Richard Crossman, Minister of Health, Niall MacDermot, Financial Secretary at the Treasury, Reg Prentice, Minister of Education and Lord Goronwy Roberts, Minister of State for Foreign Affairs.

In addition, Angela and I are both happy to spend time on the more mundane and traditional hobbies for senior citizens such as gardening and painting for leisure and we are keen members of the local Art Group where we enjoy showing our paintings at the annual exhibition. Meanwhile, I have discovered a new and previously unsuspected interest in actually sitting down and writing this autobiography. Angela insists it could be made into a fantastic film. Now perhaps there's another challenging project for me to tackle next year?

ABOUT THE AUTHOR

'Driven to Downing Street' is the life story of the longest serving Government Car Service driver, who for several years drove an armoured protection car in the company of Special Branch protection officers. Peter Smithson explains how his life progressed from humble beginnings in a miner's cottage in County Durham to his own office in No. 11 Downing Street, with friends at the highest level of Government. Determined to improve his life, the story wends its way from a childhood of poverty and little education, through deprivation and anxious times during World War 2, followed by an austere yet exciting life in the RAF in Malaya, to a gradual progression through the ranks of the Government Car Service, where he enjoyed an exciting and eventful career.

Peter offers his own unique insight into some of the most important events of that period, including the Brighton bomb, Geoffrey Howe's relationship with Margaret Thatcher, whose driver happened to be a good friend of his, and the dangers posed by the IRA. He gives a revealing 'behind the scenes' account of his time with Government ministers at the highest level, including Harold Macmillan, Sir Alec Douglas Home, Richard Crossman and Reg Prentice. He also had occasion to meet famous people such as Sir Winston Churchill and Margaret Thatcher as well as important foreign personalities including President John Kennedy, President Gorbachev and the Aga Khan. Finally, he achieved his ambition of becoming the permanent driver for the Foreign Secretary, (Sir Geoffrey Howe), who he drove for 24 years when he served in Thatcher's cabinet as Chancellor of the Exchequer, Foreign Secretary and then Deputy Prime Minister and subsequently when he entered the House of Lords. Peter was awarded the BEM and the Imperial Service Medal for meritorious service over 47 years.